I GAVE GOD TIME

Ann Kiemel Anderson

Tyndale House Publishers, Inc.
Wheaton, Illinois

Second printing, November 1982

Library of Congress Catalog Card Number 82-60244
ISBN 0-8423-1560-8
Copyright © 1982 by My Neighbor, Inc.
  All rights reserved.

Printed in the United States of America

to william earle anderson, II
my husband.
the perfect man for me.
God's choice.

with special love to
raymond berry, tom gibbon, clark peddicord—
men's men. God's men.
will's comrades.

"may the God who inspires men to endure,
and gives them a Father's care, give you a mind
united towards one another because of your
common loyalty to Jesus Christ. and then, as
one, you will sing from the heart the praises
of God the Father of our Lord Jesus Christ.
so open your hearts to one another as Christ
has opened His heart to you, and God will be
glorified."

romans 15:5-7
phillips

to dream.
to take on something great . . .
beyond oneself.
to wear my heart in my shoe
and run with it.

to face the mountain
and challenge it
and woo it
until it crumbles.
to not give up until
the sunrise dances again
on the walls and through rooms
and over tables into corners.
erupting hearts
bringing joy . . .
response.

to keep one's back straight.
to keep one's face toward the sun.
to beckon all of life to come
and follow you and the
giant God.

to long for truth.
no blur. no mist or fog.
to know life in clean, untarnished
terms.
to long for it as sun must
long for morning sky.
or dry, parched earth
and cracked
for drenching rain.

to say, "i'll wait". . .
and never pull ahead
or reach beyond
until the road is cleared
and the path smoothed.
days or years.
no doubt or fear.
to know that never-failing love
will some day
somehow
reach out to me.
and in His hand
bring the childhood
dream. the eternal
fulfillment.

     amen.

     amen.

prologue

the old claremont hotel, san francisco.
covenant ladies' conference.
i had flown in from boston to speak.
my parents, driving over from marin county, came
    for dinner at the hotel. it was my father's
    seventieth birthday.
    celebration. thanksgiving.

an old college friend, rosemary midby, came to stay
    with me that weekend. unmarried. school
    teacher from pasadena. solid. no nonsense.
    one of my most trusted persons.

after dinner and speaking. . . my parents having
    returned home. . .
    rosemary and i were sitting on separate beds
    in my hotel room. tired. in pajamas.
    facing each other.

suddenly rosemary said,
    "ann, i feel the Lord specifically spoke to me
    about you. . . ."
    "really?" i smiled. "what did He say?"
    "do you really want to know?"
    "yes. . . rosa, you aren't kidding, are you?"
    "i am serious. it was so vivid."

i could not imagine what the Lord had said.
rolling over on my stomach, head burrowed in pillow,

i waited.
"ann, Jesus seemed to say He is preparing you
for a husband."
"a husband!" i screamed. eyes shining. stunned.
"really, rosa . . . a *husband?*"
she nodded. she was serious. rosemary is someone
i *believe.*

i lay motionless. it seemed incredible . . . not even in
my realm of thinking. thirty-one years old.
on a mission to the world. alone.
my eyes were growing wet.
"do you actually believe i am going to marry
someday?"
"i do."
and for hours and days and months . . . then years . . .
i remembered. never forgot.
pondered it in my heart.
and believed.

it had been a long trip, twenty-one days on the road.
as i spoke in one place, another group called to
     ask if i could come there . . . university students
     from washington state at pullman.
people with faith and vision. so i went.

flown in by private plane.
escorted through the back stage door of the
     university's auditorium.
a feeling of electricity in the air. several thousand
     who had come together with last-minute notice that
     i was arriving.
i was tired but caught up by the enthusiasm.
my same plain message. my simple white dress.
my hair pulled up with barrettes, growing from
     the short-to-the-longer stage.
not for a moment did i realize the impact that day
     would have on my life.

julie anderson gibbon and her husband, tom, were
     in the audience to hear me. they were from
     moscow, idaho.
"will has got to meet ann," julie commented.
in anderson fashion, not about to be deterred,
     she pushed through the crowds and found
     her way backstage.
i was being whisked out, to fly immediately to my
     next appearance.

she grabbed my arm.
i was amazed by her beauty, her cameo complexion,
     her long black braids over her shoulders.
     her shining dark eyes.

julie, who prayed every day for four years
that i would meet her brother.

"ann, my sister is an artist in new york city.
she needs fellow Christians. maybe you will meet
   her sometime.
and my brother, will . . . ."

i was being pushed into the car before others could
   stop me.
hundreds of mothers with unmarried sons had told me
   they hoped i would meet their boys . . . and sisters,
   their brothers. i thought nothing of it.
only gratitude for another task completed.
another audience to whom i had delivered my
   dreams.

but julie . . . with a sense of conviction . . .
started praying every day that i would meet will.
she went to her Bible study/prayer group and shared
   this dream with them.
professors told me later that they laughed at her.
they knew this time julie had gone too far.
how could her potato-farmer brother from faraway
   idaho ever make contact with ann kiemel,
   public speaker, in boston?

for four years, julie prayed.
every single day.
when will would bring a girl home . . . or double date
   with tom and julie in moscow, julie would say,
"she is nice, will . . . but she is not like ann."
ANN!
he learned to hate that name.
he had never read my books, nor heard me speak.
who was i anyway?
whoever or whatever i was . . . he was not interested.
no woman julie picked could possibly work.

this wasn't the first time his little sister had gotten
   under his skin.
years before, will would coax julie and chrisi to get
   into the little boat with him and go out on the
   small lake. to fish. to pretend adventure.
julie would often stay on the bank, pull her knees up
   under her chin, and pray that will would make it
   back to shore safely. that the boat would not tip.
   that he would not drown.
she would call out to him and beg him to come back in.

when he was twenty-one, in college,
   he decided he was going to seek truth.
   no mixture. no blur. the absolute basics.
he would study all the religions of the world,
   collect his data, and choose.
finding an old Bible, he decided to start with
   Christianity.
every weekend, he would drop the Bible into a
   backpack, along with an apple and a candy bar.
he had often heard that fasting was an
   encouragement to spiritual understanding.
he would take a little temptation along to test his
   discipline and courage and enhance his search.

climbing a couple of miles into the mountains,
   he would stop on a rock, pull out the Bible,
   and say, "God, teach me what you want me to
   know. amen," and start reading.
genesis, exodus, leviticus, numbers.
he was getting bogged down, so he flipped over
   to the New Testament.
matthew, mark, luke, john.
"the WORD became flesh, and dwelt among us. . . ."
he did not understand.

flipping back to luke, he tried to build the
   framework for those first verses.
in quiet moments, totally alone, he chose
   to follow Jesus Christ.
in time, his sisters, julie and chrisi,
   and his mother followed too.
only after years of family prayer, on his deathbed
   with stomach cancer, did will's father
   commit his life to Jesus also.

julie sent will my *YES* book, and a poster with
   my face on it.
she tried to get him to go hear me speak when i
   appeared in pocatello, forty minutes from
   idaho falls.
(for years i had said, "i'll go anywhere Jesus sends
   me...even pocatello, idaho...but i think He
   will let me stay in boston the rest of my life."
i always used "pocatello" because it sounded so
   remote, so funny, so impossible.
   little did i know!)

november 1980

will received an energy award from a national
   organization for his work with drip irrigation.
knowing he would be coming east for the
   presentation, he decided to call boston...to
   see if he could stop and take me to dinner.
to get julie off his back.
to be able to say, "julie, i met ann.
   i bought her dinner.
   she is not for me. now get off this kick."

calling directory assistance, he got my number.
since my home number was unlisted, he was
    connected with my office.
"hello, this is will anderson calling.
may i speak to ann?"
"i am sorry, but she is unavailable. may i suggest
    you write her instead? she is usually very
    difficult to reach by phone, but she answers
    all her mail."

write her a letter? no way. he would keep calling.
eight calls later, he began to realize he was
    getting the runaround.
who was this "ann kiemel" anyway?
frustrated, he sent a telegram:

"37-YEAR-OLD POTATO FARMER WOULD
LIKE TO TAKE YOU TO DINNER, AS LONG
AS YOU DO NOT ORDER STOVE-TOP
STUFFING WITH YOUR STEAK. WILL BE IN
BOSTON NOVEMBER 22-25."

it was unique. it did catch my eye.
i had andie, my secretary, send a note, saying
    i would meet him for dinner november 23 between
    five and six-thirty.
period!

a note from the secretary!
an allotted time — merely one and a half hours
    for a dinner date!
will was amazed...disgusted. some woman!

the days passed.
meanwhile, i was trying to survive the most difficult

period of my life.
there was no thought of marriage or even romance in
    my heart. only of pain and grief.
of the sky turning black. no star on the horizon.
no hope. just my fierce, beating heart.
my disciplined spirit getting me through one day
    at a time.
pushing me out for my ten or fifteen miles along
    the charles river.
loving the neighborhood children.

november 23 arrived.
something in me rebelled. who was this
    will anderson anyway?
i could hardly cope with everything else.
how did i think i could possibly squeeze in a
    dinner with some unknown, probably
    intrusive man?

"andie, i cannot face will anderson tonight,
    whoever he is.
you stay here at the office. when he arrives, tell
    him that i am sorry i could not make the
    date, but that something has come up.
suggest that maybe we can have dinner the next time
    he is in boston.
i think i should take a pizza to the calhouns.
    you know, i have not seen them for a long time."

i was at the calhouns, twenty minutes away,
    visiting, eating greasy pizza i had brought in.
the phone rang. "ann . . . this is andie.
ann, this man is really nice. he is quality. you can tell.
he has been to the finest french restaurant in boston,
    and ordered a special meal.

tipped the maitre d'.
i feel terrible.
he says he will not be in boston for six or seven more
    years. he seems okay about your not showing,
    but . . . ."

(actually will was relieved. he hadn't wanted to
    meet me anyway.
now he could go home and tell julie he tried . . .
    it hadn't worked . . . get off his case!)

after a few moments of contemplation, i picked up
    the phone and called his hotel.
"will? ann kiemel. so sorry i had complications.
could we meet for tea around 9:30 tonight?
i'll come there."

his voice was smooth. deep. assured.
he sounded nice.
a tiny current of fascination ran through my mind.
still in running pants and a jacket, i went from
    quincy back into boston, and arrived at
    the hotel a few minutes past 9:30.
running into the lobby, i caught sight of him
    immediately.
he was sitting in an easy chair — engrossed in a book.
(i have seen him that way hundreds of times since.)
dark suit . . . khaki overcoat . . . curly black hair.
when he looked up, his dark eyes seemed to penetrate
    clear through me.
pleasant smile . . . energy. all kinds of energy flowing
    through and around him.

i did not really care what he thought. i was just
    carrying out an obligation.

he was not at all interested in how i felt, either.
it was a necessary task to be completed so julie would
    abandon her constant harping about "ann."
because of this mutual indifference we were both
    relaxed. natural. comfortable.
"ann, i have never been stood up before. and i was
    not about to miss the best meal in town,
    so i called the maitre d' and told him i would
    come alone, as i had been stranded." he smiled.
    "there is a little cafe down the street.
    shall we go?"

something miraculous happened at that moment.
for years, i had felt uncomfortable putting my arm
    in a man's. either we were not matching heights . . .
    or for some other reason it didn't feel good.
i liked spontaneity. a man grabbing my hand.
    reaching out and wrapping his arm around my
    neck.
holding me by the belt loop on my skirt or jeans.
nothing staid . . . or stiff . . . or formal.
blowing a kiss with one finger . . . or kissing the back
    of the hand.
reaching up and tracing a quiet path on one cheek.
winking across the table. turning unexpectedly and
    giving a quick, tight squeeze . . . then letting
    loose and going on.
i did not like too much protocol . . . too much cool,
    detached, "this-is-how-it-is-done" stuff.
here's the miraculous part:
in my heart, never telling anyone in the whole world,
    i had decided that the man who reached out
    and grabbed my arm and directed *me* would be
    my man.
will anderson did exactly that.

holding my arm, he led me through the hotel lobby.
we walked that way down the street to the cafe.
he was confident. . . assured. . . in charge.
he walked fast, briskly. no nervous laugh.
no fast or cute talk. in control.
animated, but in a casual way.
interested, yet not very.
we ordered hot chocolate instead of tea.
he became serious and said, "i would like to
    tell you about me."
no nonsense.

he spoke of julie. about graduating from the
    university of utah. of going to the university
    of idaho for graduate work, and studying for
    six months in new zealand.
he talked about potatoes. . . and politics. . . and the
    power of prayer.
he mentioned his intention of going to israel to
    study "drip irrigation" with government
    authorities.
no excess of words. no pretense. no attempt to
    impress or spiritualize. just matter-of-fact.
    warm. detached. honest. i was amazed.
i had an idea.

"will, in one month i am taking seven high school and
    college girls to israel with my road man and me. i
    am going to run the israeli marathon again
    this year.
i have been praying for another man to go along,
    for security.
it's a long trip, and i think we need the extra
    help and protection.
since you have traveled the world. . . and are planning

to go anyway . . . why not go a little earlier,
    with us?
you could study and meet with officials . . . and join us
    in the evening.''

he seemed amazed that i should toss out such an
    invitation when just two hours before, i had
    stood him up for a dinner date.
frankly, it was spontaneous. impulsive.
the conversation drifted to other things . . . the trip
    was not mentioned again.
after an hour and a half of visiting, he dropped me at
    my apartment.

''good night, ann. see you — here, there, or in the
    air . . . .''

oh, how corny, i thought. what a strange statement.
nice man . . . but an *idaho potato farmer*. not my type.
i forgot all about his taking my arm, and i began to
    grapple with all the issues facing me.
if i married, it would have to be to a polished, smooth,
big-city man. preferably a bostonian.
this was my city . . . my calling.
i was here to stay.
will would tell julie, ''i met her. she is nice,
    but not my type. too skinny. no real
    curves.
just not what i have waited thirty-seven years for!''

somehow, though, years before . . . i must have been
    with julie and chrisi, back on the sandy rim of
    that little lake . . . squinting my eyes against
    afternoon sun, straining to see him. to find
    him. to keep his little boat in sight, far
    out on the lake.

i must have been calling out. . .urging him to come
  back. . .praying he would not be so reckless, so
  careless. so brave. so unafraid.
praying he would make it back to shore.
somehow i must have known that some day he would
  be my man and i his woman. . .wooing him for
  all the sunrises of the tomorrows.

flashback

as i prepared for the trip to israel, my mind kept
  exploring the memories from the previous year's
  jaunt. . .and my first israeli marathon.
twelve small, amazing children. . .mostly from
  boston's different corners.
  pablo. joseph. charlie. ashley.
nine adults to help me. the berrys. joanne ferguson.
  the fishers. bev and cindy to run the marathon with
  me. steve. all special people. . .my guests.
for all of us, the first trip to israel.
wayne coombs and stan reilly went too. . .they were
  the producer and director of the documentary film
  being made about my life. the film crew were
  israelis, and met us over there.

i ran the marathon. we shared Christmas in
  jerusalem.
i was featured on israeli television and became known
  all over that small country as the "marathon lady."
i hugged the children, held them on my lap, sang
  them little songs. we ate, laughed, and cried
  together.
we visited all the magnificent old places where Jesus
  lived and walked.

when the group returned to america, i flew on to rome
with the film crew to do more footage, running the
appian way. i had police escorts, chauffeurs,
royal care.
then nonstop to san francisco. . . i arrived at my
parents' in time to celebrate new year's eve
with the entire family.
i was animated. secure. reinforced by people's love
and attention.
i was lean and solid and strong.
i had faced the mountain. . . accomplished one
marathon. . . and was excited and committed
to another.

1980, a long year

"teach me to die, Lord. . . teach me. . .
so that in dying, i can live. . . ."
several things happened in 1980. finishing the
gymnasium for children in boston's north end.
hiring a full-time director to run it.
never asking for money, but using my own and
any other money that came in.

then, the documentary film on my life.
a big chunk of my book money was invested in
this project so as to have some control
over its production.
then problems. . . every month being called for
more money. silver prices going up. . . more
lab splicing. . . delays.

i was not a business woman. i had never even
pretended to be.

i watched the money i had always used for
neighborhood projects dissipate. the labs
were taking longer than usual with the
films.
the editing was more difficult . . . more complex
than was expected.
some days i did not even have money to pay my
employees . . . nor money for my food . . . or to
buy a child ice cream.
or to pay my insurance.
the world got bigger and scarier. i became smaller and
more trapped. more tangled in a web from which
i couldn't free myself.
it's too complex to tell, but it is enough to say that
day by day i felt myself being slowly,
fiercely, sucked under.

i would fly to a speaking engagement, and . . . as
never before . . . the sponsor would apologize . . .
saying he was short of money and could not
fulfill his agreement.
sometimes when i came into my office, the accountant
would be there with a sober look on his face.
taxes were due. no money to pay them.

throughout, i never asked for a dime.
though people to whom i was close would advise me
to ask, i could not . . . it was not my way.
it was not that i was too proud, but i really believed
God was my Source. if He wanted to use other
people's money to help me, He could speak to
them directly.
in a few desperate moments, when i was tempted to
call someone (for i knew many would have been

happy to lend me money if they had known of
my plight),
i felt definitely it would have been a human
response rather than one of quiet faith and
waiting on God.

there have been other dark, agonizing places in my
life. black, hollow echoes to my broken,
pleading heart.
but i know of nothing that tests one's basic character
so severely as financial crisis. of knowing, every
day, that if God does not deliver, then everything
you have worked and stood for is totally lost . . .
and you are finished. your work. your hopes
and dreams.
are you going to stand straight? or compromise?
or choose easier, faster answers than God's?
can you be happy and loving and giving and caring
when your very foundation is shaking?
is your joy built into the sovereign, magnificent Christ or your own achievement?
was i willing to relinquish? to trust?
where had i failed?
never . . . absolutely never . . . had i felt i had placed
value in money. it seemed to be the purest place
in my life.
i lived to give it away. i worked hard to have it
to spend on others.
but God knows the secret ways of the heart.
the private deceit. the hidden pride.
the hidden securities . . . other than Himself . . .
in our lives.
His love compels Him to purge us. to purify the
covered-over places.
my desire in life was to be *His* . . . to do His will.

through the dark, i screamed and cried and
ached and hurt. . . and prayed for grace.
grace greater than all this.

one night in particular, knowing that the next day
some bills had to be paid, i found myself
kneeling by my bed, crying.
after a few moments, i got up, found a paper and pen,
and wrote out four ways this money could come in:
1. my father might get a loan for me.
(i had never asked him for that.)
2. i could ask friends.
3. i could use raymond's investment he had
offered.
4. a miracle could happen.
laying the paper aside, i got down on my face next to
the bed, thinking that if i lay face-down, it
would be the best position in which to be
humble. . . the Lord would hear me.
"Jesus, i must have money. i only want it to
glorify You. to love my neighborhood. to be a
good representative of Your grace.
if you do not send me money, i will go under. . . ."

He seemed to answer:
"ann, do not *ever* ask Me for more money.
I am a Millionaire. i own the cattle on a
thousand hills. i will always give you everything
you need from day to day.
you do not need money. you need more of Me.
pray for more of *Me* in your life. . . ."

how simple and plain. how true. no blur. no haze.
no watering-down. an absolute — one of the few.
more of Jesus. . . that was all i would ever need.

the next morning, after getting up at 5:30 and having
    devotions, i pulled on my running clothes.
    the sky was dark and the ground wet and cold.
i started out, on nothing but gut determination, to
    see old jock.
jock, my incredible Scotsman who directs the boston
    marathon, and takes care of the bruins
    and the celtics. my great friend.
    he would massage my sore legs, and i would
    tell him about Jesus.

    "ann, ye look so skinny. ye doin' okay?
    ye makin' it, aren't ye?"

    "yeah, jock . . . i'm doing all right. . . ."
but somehow the tears could not be stopped . . .
    nor the pain.
    "well, jock, i know i am *going* to make it,
    but money has been real tight, and sometimes i
    get pretty scared.
    today is one of those deadlines, and i am so beat,
    trying to face deadlines. it's lonely and tough."

    "how much ye need?"

    "oh, too much for you to help.
    Jesus will take care of it."

by four o'clock that evening, i had run twelve
    miles . . .
    visited neighborhood families . . . answered
    mail . . . and then i came into my office.
    my heart was racing . . . a dull ache in my chest.
    it was down to the wire, no miracles.
    no bundle of money left at my door, like all the

stories i had heard.
i saw my accountant from downtown, sitting there
   with a despairing look.
     "ann, it looks pretty serious."

i thought i detected tears in his eyes. he had
   taken care of my finances for a couple of years.
   he had seen me with a lot. . . now with nothing.
though i think he had not started out as a strong
   believer, he had heard all my little songs. . . i
   prayed with him every single time he came by.
   i had told him about Jesus. . . had squeezed his
   hand.
   his wife had even invited me for dinner.
   a camaraderie had developed.

   "i know, dick." i turned so he would not see
   my tears coming.
   "i guess i will have to call some people to see
   if they can lend me some money. you know, dick, i
   have never believed in asking *anyone* but God. . .
   but maybe i am wrong. . . ."
my voice drifted. going to my desk, i started to pick
   up the phone.

   "ann, there is something i thought about.
   you have a retirement program you have been
   paying into. with some penalty, you could
   withdraw the funds, and it would help us."

i wheeled around, excitement blazing in my eyes.
   "dick, could we? oh, that is the miracle!
   i would not have to ask anyone. . . and i don't
   need retirement money anyway."

the next day, in the mail, there came a check from jock
    for a very sizable amount. it was beyond
    my comprehension.
    i knew this man . . . he was scotch.
    he was thrifty . . . he watched every penny.
    i was overwhelmed.

months came and went. i saved and saved until i
    could pay jock back, although there was no
    stipulation on his part.
    that crisis was past. Jesus met my need.
    i only had to go to Him. He never failed.
i began to trust Him as never before.

one day, as i had changed planes in chicago's o'hare
    airport, an older man had come up to me.
"aren't you ann kiemel?"

"yes. . . ."

"i am stanley tam. i have looked forward to meeting
    you."
he was on my flight, going to the same city as i.
shortly after take-off, he moved back to the seat next
    to mine. knowing he had written a book entitled
    God owns my business, i felt led to ask
    his advice.
    whatever had i done wrong with my finances?
"ann, God is your Source. just look up and cut a hole
    in the ceiling, wherever you are, and go directly
    to Him. He is your Father. He owns everything.
    you never need to tell anyone else. He will always
    hear you . . . ."

for a couple of hours, on that DC-10, i would lean
    back and look up to the ceiling of the plane.
mentally, i would keep cutting a hole, look at the sky,
    and start talking to my Father.

"oh, Lord . . . i cry out to You. i am your struggling
    child. i trust You. i need You. Lord, do You
    really see me here?"

before we parted, stanley said,
"ann, there is a place of stretch in everyone's life.
even if you have plenty of money, someone you love
    may be sick or suffering.
often poor people have great children . . . and
    corporation presidents may have children in
    conflict with the law . . . or a retarded child.
everyone has problems. it draws us to God.
it mellows and humbles and refines us.
face today's need, and let God work through it."

we landed in washington, and he was gone.
i would never forget that encounter.

i gave God time . . . and room and space.
he worked to create in me, His child,
    a more quiet, centered place.
    a deeper root of peace and trust.
    He never fails to come through.

it is never money that is the issue . . .
    only more of Him.
    and time.

late december 1980

now it was a year later.
i returned to israel to run the marathon again.
five marathons under my belt by now.
my road man and a newly-met "will anderson" to
    help us.
plus seven lovely teen-age girls.
a year ago i had personally paid for twenty-one people
    to go. twelve months later i didn't have enough
    money to pay my own way, not to mention anyone
    else's.

the israeli travel agency had sent tickets for two
    (i took tim, my new road man, because he was
    a marathoner too). this was a gesture in response
    to the big business from the year before.
the seven girls paid their own ways so they could go
    with us.

i was a different ann.
my eyes were quiet. i was too skinny.
the pain and confusion of the previous months had left
    me empty. without energy.
i wondered about my giant God. about dreams.
(teach me to die, Lord . . . teach me . . .
so that in dying, i can live . . . .)

my second trip to israel was the greatest experience
    of my life.
though i had nothing, i had everything.
the previous year, there had been too many cameras,
    too much pressure and activity connected with
    running my first israeli marathon, to let me
    really appreciate that miraculous little country.

this year my life was empty . . . cleaned out . . .
    purified.
my hungry eyes and anxious heart searched for every
    scrap of blessing to be found.

i absorbed every pebble and worn jewish face and
    color in the sky and word spoken by the guide.
i looked for Jesus and for Truth in every village,
    every story, every handshake. i hungered and
    thirsted and was filled.
i smelled the air that Jesus breathed. i could hear
    His footsteps. i could see the fishermen on the
    sea of galilee with new understanding.
i felt bathed by the sunshine . . . transformed.
i longed for God's presence as the new day longs for
    the morning sun.

the high school and college girls i had taken with me
    were wonderful.
tim and i ran the marathon in cold and rain and
    sometimes mud and water to our ankles. i tore
    a muscle at the fifteenth mile . . . but we
    finished. we celebrated.
will ran eighteen miles of the twenty-six
    before an ambulance picked him up.
    so fatigued. his only fear was that he *wouldn't* die.
    smile.

during the day will studied farming techniques and
    drip irrigation with government officials, and
    joined us in the evening for dinner.
he did special things for the girls . . . surprise birthday
    parties. cold drinks along the way.
however, i felt no romantic inclination toward him.
    (what did he know? he was still from idaho.)

he continued to feel the same about me. *(nice
woman. . .caring. . .but too skinny and fragile.)*

we were still in israel on new year's eve. i asked tim
and will to awaken all of us thirty minutes before
midnight, so we could have communion together
and welcome in the new year.
i was ready for a fresh calendar. . .a new beginning.
with no regret, i bade farewell to 1980 with all its
stress and pain.
as each of us shared with the others in that small hotel
room in jerusalem, the Spirit of God came to us.
never before had i been so vulnerable. . .but i felt led
to open up. . .
"i have always believed in dreams. i thought i was
strong. . .invincible. i resented weakness. . .
denied it. have worked all my life to prove
it was not a part of me.
this last year, however, i have realized how imperfect
i am.
along with the entire human race, i am weak.
Jesus is my only Hope.
i have been poor. . .have actually been hungry.
i know what it is to be scared.
tonight, i am no longer the self-assured, brave
person i once was. . .but i am running my
race to the end.
i am not getting off. . .not quitting.
i am living out all i committed myself to in my
YES book. . .to hurt, pain, loss, death.
tonight, i still know YES pays. it leads me to the
finish line.
i am running straight to the end, even if i have
had to crawl part way."

i choked out the words. i wept.
the seven impressionable young girls listened . . .
  watched.
i didn't want to be a hero . . . i wanted only to be real.
to be a pilgrim on the right journey.
never to lose sight of the one quiet Star on the
  horizon.
i had nothing to prove but God's grace.

as i started to fall into bed — more emotionally
  drained than physically tired, there was a
  knock at my hotel room door.
it was will, dark eyes flashing.
''ann, thanks for being so honest tonight. i have been
  where you are — in spades. my father died of
  cancer five years ago, and left the whole business
  on my young shoulders.
dad had said he had two regrets: that i had never
  known the great depression, or the experience of
  being dead broke.
that either one makes a man out of a boy.
shortly after he died, the business nearly went under.
where once i had all the answers . . . was critical of
  other farmers' crooked potato rows and irrigation
  procedures . . . i would now lie face down on the
  floor, crying for strength and mercy simply
  to survive.
ann, i know how tough that can be. thanks again for
  sharing.''

two days later, just before we left israel, everyone
  wanted to be baptized.
though i had been immersed years before, i decided to

join the group because this was israel, and these
were "my" girls.
we called a nazarene missionary from nazareth, and
we all headed for the sea of galilee. we chose to
go there rather than to the jordan river, so
muddy and dirty.

the sky was flawlessly clear. the fishermen were
casting nets in the distance, just as they had
2,000 years ago.
the sun streamed across the silvery-smooth water . . .
warm on our hair and necks.
we sang a few hymns and then began to walk out into
the frigid, numbing water. i was last in line, so
i could watch tim and the girls in front of me.
will was en route to meetings, but stood on the shore
and participated with us from a distance.

the radiant faces . . . the music being carried across
the water . . . wet heads . . . cold, shivering
bodies . . . fast-beating, eager, open hearts.
before pastor hunter immersed me, i looked around at
the shivering little group.
"when i come up, i want you to sing,
freely, freely, you have received . . .
freely, freely give.
go in My Name, and because you believe,
others will know that I live.
sing that song for me . . . . "

the hanky was placed over my nose and a strong
arm across my back. then i felt that clean,
cold water washing over me.

and i will give you a new heart —

i will give you new and right desires —
and put a new spirit within you.
i will take out your stony hearts of sin
and give you new hearts of love.
and i will put my Spirit within you so that you
will obey my laws and do whatever i command.
                    ezekiel 36:26, 27

suddenly my head was back up. i was breathing the
    air.
everything was new, clean. old things washed away.
the sun was shining in my eyes, on my face.
i was changed. different heart. . . new hope.
the voices were singing all around me,
    "freely. . .freely. . . ." i was singing too.
they were reaching for me. . . hugging me.
i didn't know why i was crying. . . i couldn't stop.
nothing would ever be the same.

i carried a new treasure of freedom in my heart.
no words. no tongues. just freedom.
the sins of my youth. the dreariness of the past year.
    the weakness and imperfection of this human
    clay. . . all cleansed.

forever i will remind the world, Jesus carries the
    heavy burden. lifts the load. clears the path.
as we give God time, he changes *everything*.
as long as i live, i will sing that song
    and keep the music moving to all the corners
    of the earth. . . to every listening heart.

dietrich bonhoeffer said it:
    cheap grace is grace we bestow upon
    ourselves — grace without discipleship.

costly grace is the gospel that must be sought
again and again. the gift which must be asked for.
the door at which a man must knock. it is costly
because it cost a man his life and it is grace
because it gives a man the only true life.

from ann to will
    january 12, 1981
    dear will. . .
thank you for listening and not being defensive.
for running behind me in the marathon and praying.
for lindy's birthday cake. . . and our extraordinary
    and wonderful dinner at the hilton.
thank you for rubbing my sore, pained muscles.
for being open and honest and frank.
for working with the girls.

thank you for coming to israel with the teenagers
    and tim and me. . . and fitting in so well.
for being a man of integrity and trust and discipline
    and character.
i know Jesus is with us. . . and i can run all the
    miles, to the end, saying "YES" to anything,
    if He is there.

love and joy and blessing. . .

                                  ann

from ann to will
    january 14, 1981
    will, good morning:
i'm looking forward, if it falls into place,
    to idaho. . . and skiing. . . and being with you.

i would not feel right staying more than six days
  or so. we can talk about that later.
the time off the road . . . away from speaking . . .
  will be good.

i do not know all the things i feel. i am still
  guarded.
and i'm surprised (as i am sure you are) at this
  relationship . . . but i do respect, more and more,
  the character and qualities i see in you.
thanks for not taking advantage of me . . . or trying to.
for accepting that i am a public person.
for not denying it . . . but for working at not letting
  it intimidate you.

pondering many things in my heart . . .

                                                    ann

from ann to will
  january 20, 1981
  dear will . . .
your letter came today . . . about who we are apart
  from our achievements . . . about my being
  vulnerable to a relationship because of my
  situation. sensitive. very touching.
you are relating to me as a woman.
you are inspiring me to prayer.
you continue to exhibit that you are truly God's . . .
  and that His character is being implanted in you.

what you implied is right . . . we need to know each other . . .
  at risk . . . much better. that will increasingly
  unfold to us what this relationship is purposed to
  achieve.

today i have eaten fruit, one egg, two and a half muffins,
seven cookies, a half can of almonds, and some
macaroni and cheese. CAN YOU BELIEVE THAT!
sighhhh. i must change.
will, i continue to be amazed that a man of your
character exists. . . at thirty-seven years of age.
you have a wonderful future. God is going to bless
your business. i really believe that.

every day, i understand better. . . Jesus is the only
good thing in me. He, only, makes my life
valuable. . . with purpose.
i love Him.
i feel like a small girl. . . searching. . . watching. . .
following, with open, trusting heart. and
with a pure, great love. wanting to trace all
His steps, and stay close to Him.

love,
ann

january 1981

i had been back from israel less than a month.
will called and invited me to join him and some
    family and friends on a skiing trip.
    he said he would send a ticket.
it so happened i was to make a television appear-
    ance in seattle the weekend before the
    skiing trip, so i suggested i just stop in
    idaho en route home to boston. it would not
    cost me extra, nor will.

i was *not* romantically interested in will anderson,
    but skiing is always exhilarating, and

cross-country style is a wonderful workout
   for marathon training. it would be a
   diversion. i could spare the days.
why not?

following my tv interview, i returned to the hotel.
it was late. as i got ready for bed, i began to
   realize i was *terrified* to go to idaho the
   next morning.
never in my life had i really, seriously, opened my
   life to a man. i had dated many. some i
   thought i loved. i had had flirtations . . . friendships.
but will anderson was different. he was available . . .
   never married . . . a strong believer . . . the right
   age . . . healthy . . . straight arrow . . . clean
   history . . . trustworthy.
this man might be a potential candidate.
it came to me more and more that all the other
   men i had known were not ones to whom
   i could open my whole life.
basically, i have always been a free spirit . . .
   vulnerable . . . trusting . . . open.
unashamed to say, "this is who i am."
i felt comfortable with men . . . spoke on the same
   platforms with them . . . traveled with them . . .
   spent hours in conversation.
but it was something else to let anyone, apart from
   my twin sister, jan, know me through and through.
   to unveil the deepest parts of me . . . to show
   my scars, my wounds, my weaknesses, my fears.
to let a man really know me . . . .

i was shaken by a fear i could not control. it came
   to me that i had never let anyone come that
   close.

what if a man really knew me? how would he feel
    when he realized i was so imperfect?
all my life i had suffered from the childhood rejections
    handed to me from the outside world.
i was not pretty. . .not exciting. . . not worthy.
for years i tried carefully to see to it that those
    painful feelings never came again.
i could never let anyone reject me like that again.

"jan," i wept into the phone. "i just *can't* go to
    idaho tomorrow. i'm afraid to meet will's
    family. . .to know him better. i am scared!"
my sister. . .in cleveland. . .my best friend.
a well-trained psychologist. warm, easy, reassuring.
"ann, you will have fun. go just for that — to have
    a good time. to ski. it does not have to
    be anything more."

as i fell into bed, i had a strange new feeling.
i suddenly realized that going to idaho was an
    adventure unlike any other in my life.
outwardly i denied any real meaning or purpose
    behind this trip. . .
but subconsciously i must have known there was a
    plan-in-the-making.

at three a.m. i was still awake. i had not slept at all.
finally i picked up the phone again and called
    armand, a dear friend in boston. . .
    a giant Christian.
i had known and respected him several years.
we had spent hours talking about life and reality
    and about some of my feelings and convictions.
it would be six a.m. now in boston. i could wait
    no longer.

his daughter, kim, answered the phone.
"kim, it is ann kiemel. is your dad up yet?"

"yes, but he has been real sick with the flu.
i think he can talk, though. hang on."

"ann?"...armand's warm, reassuring voice.

"oh, armand, i am sorry to call so early...but i am
    beside myself. i am en route to idaho to ski
    with this will anderson i told you about.
it is very strange, but i am very scared. i just
    do not know how i can do it...."
again i was crying.

"ann, what time is it there?"

"three a.m."

he laughed spontaneously. i could almost hear him
    think, "my word, this child should be asleep."
he encouraged me to go on with my visit — as jan
    had done.
whatever did i have to fear? i didn't have to marry
    anyone i didn't want to.
after skiing and good food and warm chatter,
    i could fly home and choose whether or not to
    speak to this man ever again.
true. yes, that was right.
what was i getting so worked up over?
i was an independent woman...secure...
    professional.
unswayed by *any* man. certainly not by a potato
    farmer from idaho.
i remembered some of our conversations in israel.

we had had several evenings free to talk. the girls
   were playing games or reading in their rooms.
will anderson was a data collector. he asked everybody
   everything.
he wanted information . . . about life . . . products . . .
   jewelry . . . food . . . lifestyles . . . government.
he knew more about everything than anyone i had
   ever known.
i liked intellectual men, but i thought he carried
   thirst for knowledge too far!
he would ask me questions about marriage. about my
   attitudes toward sex. about my family background. about my health.
as for himself, he was thirty-seven years old.
   he had never slept with anyone.
   he believed in purity, and he believed a couple
   should spend time talking and becoming real
   friends before marriage, rather than getting
   involved in *any* kind of physical
   relationship.
i look back and realize how the world's perspective
   had influenced me. i certainly was God's and
   completely Christian, but i had mingled with
   so many different kinds of people. most of the
   men i had known were "city slickers."
even those who claimed Jesus Christ as Lord seemed
   to believe that some degree of intimacy was
   important.
perhaps will was too radical. too straight . . . totally
   unexciting. (was he normal? i didn't want
   to marry a man with some hidden problem.)
now, as i confess these thoughts, on paper, i
   am embarrassed and ashamed. i know now
   how totally mistaken i was.

on that cold january morning, i boarded a plane
   in seattle, bound for salt lake city.
    changing planes there, we continued to
    pocatello, and then on to idaho falls.
i had raced into the restroom at the salt lake airport. i looked terrible. no pizzazz. will
    probably would not find me exciting at all.
i was still frightened. . . but why did i care, anyway?
i was ann kiemel, my own woman. i was not interested
   in a potato farmer.

as the plane started its descent into idaho falls,
   i felt a unique panic. . . unmatched by anything
    i had ever known. . . impossible to define.

deboarding, i looked around. he was nowhere in
   sight.
i slipped through the crowd, relieved.
raced into the women's restroom for another glimpse
   of myself. . . hoped to be reassured, but instead
   felt more insecure.
for years now i had felt pretty secure emotionally,
   intellectually, socially. but my physical
   appearance had always brought a feeling of
   sadness. i felt i could never measure up.
as i pulled my bags off the moving belt, i suddenly
   saw will drive up in his green and white
   pickup.
he looked sharp. dark wool sport coat. that curly
   dark hair.
he started to shake my hand and then reached out and
   gave me a quick, easy hug.
throwing my bags in the back of the truck, he opened
   my door and helped me crawl in. *never* had i
   ridden in a pickup before.

and his was not the only one . . . it seemed that
    everyone in this town drove pickups.
amazing! strange!

i was relieved that the initial welcoming encounter
    was over. the trauma was past.
on the radio, president reagan was giving one of his
    first speeches since his inauguration.
suddenly i felt comfortable . . . and happy to be next
    to this man.

he told me he lived with his mother at the "home
    place."
he had moved there a couple of years before, to help
    make it less lonely for her in that large
    house, and to learn from his mom.
there was a house boy living there also.

"ann, i do not care what people say about my being
    this age, and still living at home.
i know it is God's program, so i am doing it."
driving to his home from the airport, i wondered
    what it would be like. after all, this
    man was virtually a stranger to me.
i had spent an hour and a half with him in boston
    in november, and ten days in israel, most of
    which time he was occupied with business and i
    was with my road man and the group of girls.
he had talked about being a "dirt farmer." for all
    i knew, he and his mother might live in some
    sad little shack, where his mother fed chickens.
    and pigs wandered under the bedroom windows.
will went tearing into a circular drive and stopped
    in front of a big old white colonial house
    with large pillars . . . weeping willows . . . birch trees.

the home place . . . big rooms, big windows, a lot of acreage. much love.

i was utterly amazed by what i saw.
an old dog, "blue," came moseying over to greet us.
will informed me that his mother taught math and
    science and was still at school.
we walked in the front door and i saw the biggest
    living room i had ever seen. walls of glass . . . a
    magnificent fireplace covering one end . . . a grand
    piano tucked into a corner.

"will, who has done all these fantastic art pieces?"

"oh, my sister chrisi. she is an artist in new york
    city. teaches at three universities and does
    exhibits."

"will's mother, jo, had placed fresh flowers —
    even in january — and fruit and a note
    in my charming little room upstairs.
i realized that will was not deprived, socially
    or otherwise.
however, if he had driven me to a shanty and told
    me i would have to help him slop the hogs . . .
    and if i had know this was God's plan for
    me . . . i would have said "YES." the real
    issue in my life was making sure i was running
    God's race for me.

three years ago, when i wrote *YES,* i made all the
    statements i was willing to live and die by.
they were not written on paper lightly.
they were founded on utter sincerity.
in the past three years, i had been learning what it
    meant to live out all i had committed to . . .
        YES to *anything.*
especially during the past year i had become more

and more aware of the fact that Jesus was
   everything.
i was going on with Him . . . it just didn't matter
   where . . . even if it was to idaho to marry
   will anderson.
i had flown to idaho that day out of sheer obedience,
   knowing this was ordered by God. the timing
   perfect . . . not knowing anything about will or
   his family.
i knew only about the YES to the Lord i served.
i confess it was a comfort to discover he was a
   gentleman farmer. not quite such a shock to my
   sissy, city ways.

his mother arrived . . . she was amazingly youthful . . .
   brilliant . . . refined . . . attractive . . . articulate.
   a wonderful cook and hostess.

each evening will and i spent hours, long after his
   mother had gone to bed, talking in front
   of a huge roaring fire.
i took long runs on the country roads around the home
   place. instead of the charles river and MIT
   and honking, screeching cars, i saw only
   endless miles of quiet fields, and horses grazing.
when i came in, shivering from the cold, will would
   have the sauna heated and the whirlpool full
   and hot.

we needed those few days alone to give us time to get
   acquainted. soon we were to meet clark
   peddicord, will's college roommate and head of
   campus crusade for Christ in germany, and his
   wife ann.

my creative, amazing, lovely mother-in-law,
jo anderson.

also will's sister julie and her husband, tom.
we were headed for McCall to ski.

i discovered that will could be a terrible dresser.
coming into the kitchen in the morning, he would
   be wearing some old double-knit polyester
   plaid pants with wide bottoms . . . with a
   clashing striped tee shirt. ugly!
i have always put value on how someone looked.
i would stand there and look at him and think,
   "Lord, this man is not my idea of a
   husband. he has no style. but Your
   love has followed me all my life, so if
   this is part of that perfect plan for me,
   YES to it . . . ."
i found myself looking only at his face . . . into
   his eyes. i would just ignore the clothes.

it was the third day of my visit . . . the next day we
   would be going to McCall . . . and he still had not
   tried to kiss me. most men i had to try
   to hold off, but not will.

"will, are you ever going to kiss me? this bothers
   me."

he roared with laughter. "give me time. just
   give me time." and he smiled.

"Jesus," i whispered, "is *this* the man You have made
   me wait thirty-five years for? if i didn't
   trust You totally, i would never accept this."

little did i realize that will was thinking similar

thoughts about me...
"Lord, she really doesn't have much of a figure...
    and i never wanted to marry someone well-
    known...someone who has made as much money
    in her lifetime as i have...someone who
    has never camped out or climbed mountains.
    and she doesn't know a thing about farming."
(smile. Jesus must have loved it.)

the secret throughout was that we were both obedient.
we were listening to God's voice...not our own.
we were giving Him time, and putting no confidence
    in what we personally thought or felt.

we drove to boise and joined the others, then we
    all headed for McCall and the beautiful cabin
    which had been loaned to us by friends of will,
    clark, and ann.
the snow was piled high...a roaring fire kept
    nourished...the frozen lake out our back door.
i was the first one out every morning.
will would run five or six miles with me, and then
    the others would come along and we would head for
    the cross-country trails.
though will and julie are great downhill skiers,
    i wanted to do only cross-country skiing, because
    i was training for the boston marathon in april,
    and i didn't want to risk injuries.

"will, i want to ski until the sun goes down and
    there is nothing left in me. please...."

little did i know the vitality and energy and
    strength of will anderson!
after everyone else was totally exhausted and had

returned to the warm, cozy cabin, will and i
would still be far away.
my fearless, tireless leader would be calling me to
follow him off the marked trails. . . through woods
and over hills and around corners.
with his wool hat pulled down over his head, and
wool knickers and sweaters keeping his 6′2½″
frame warm, he would sing all his old fraternity
songs to me.
even the silent, snow-covered branches all around us
must have smiled at the funny songs.
i would scream for him not to go so fast.

as the sun went down, we would start across the frozen
lake, heading for the far side. . . watching for the
bright scarf julie had tied on a pole so we could
tell which cabin was ours.
i would turn to watch the tracks we were making
across the ice. . . no one else had been out on the
lake at all.
we would plan what we would do if we hit a shallow
place and fell through.
when my fingers got numb with cold, will would have
me take my gloves off and tuck my icy hands inside
his sweater, in his armpits. i would look up into
his handsome, square face.
"dear God, i think i am falling in love with this man."

the sun would be setting. . . our shadows growing
longer and longer on the lake.
by the time we got to the cabin. . . miles across the
expanse of ice. . . it was dark.
again the next morning, when it was still dark,
we would creep out of our rooms. . . sleepy
but determined.

cross-country skiing with my great, strong, outdoorsman
husband.

layered with all the wool and flannel we could
   pull on, we would start out on our skiis . . .
   to the middle of the lake . . . to watch the sun
   come up over the mountains. to see the
   ice glistening as if covered by diamonds.
the sky was so blue . . . so clean . . . so clear,
   the white snow so unscarred . . . so perfect . . .
   that i felt tears on my pink, icy cheeks.

the heavens declare the glory of God,
   and the firmament showeth His handiwork . . .

i would chase will. he would chase me.
   designs in the ice. our very own signatures
   on the untouched, dazzling earth.
"let's sing," i'd call.

"okay . . . what?"

"God loves you and i love you . . . ."

"okay . . . ."

our voices were lost against the wind . . . the words
   blown away, carrying their hope and power to the
   tall, quiet mountain peaks.

will anderson had kissed me for the first time on
   a clear sunny afternoon, in the living room at
   the home place.
"i wanted to kiss you in broad daylight.
   nothing hidden. i am who i am.
   you are you.
besides, 'colors seen by candlelight
   often differ by day.' "

and somewhere along those snow-covered paths
   at McCall, i fell in love with this
   incredible creature who was so totally at home
   in the outdoors. . .
   absolutely fearless. . . skilled. . . almost
   superhuman.

the last night before we left we asked clark and ann
   to put together some questions for us. . .
   that we needed some direction. . . some counsel.
as we drove down the mountain the next day they
   asked us many specific things. . .
"why do you think you might be right for each
   other?"
"what makes you feel you could fulfill God's
   purposes in each other's lives?"
"what does each of you think would be the most
   difficult thing to accept about the other?"

we thought. shared. were boldly honest.
we were suddenly very keenly aware of a Presence in
   the car. . . a Spirit hovering over us.

clark — intellectual, strong — turned around from
   the front seat and said, "ann, i know will
   anderson better than any man on the face of
   the earth.
i think if anyone can handle you, he can."
(when clark speaks, i listen. . . i do not take
   it lightly.)
"one other thing. if you two feel it is God's plan
   for you to marry. . . and it surely seems right. . .
   i think you should do it soon.
your lives are both so unusual, so complicated,
   that if you don't do it soon, you never will."

i looked over at will anderson...
   this big, strong, sober, determined man sitting
   next to me.
for the first time it was so clear...so obvious.
this was God's man for me...His perfect choice in
   all the world.
he was the one i had waited for, these thirty-five years.

i buried my face in my hands, and could not stop
   crying.
it was overwhelming.
could i relinquish everything i loved to be this man's
   wife?
   ...my profession
   ...my heart's deep love for boston?
could i move to a remote little place like idaho falls?
could Jesus use me there?
what about the gymnasium in boston's north end?
what would my family say?
my friends?

we rode in silence while i wept out all the earnest,
   excited, frightened, fragile, feminine feelings
   of my heart.
will only put his arm around me and held me...
   seeming to understand that this decision was
   bigger than he or i. it was larger than life
   itself.
it was God's.
...God calling him to take on a woman, laden with
   a mission in the world.
...God calling me to trust my life and dreams to
   this man who had been faithful...
   uncompromising...trustworthy...for
   thirty-seven years of waiting.

we stayed that night in the home of friends in boise.
  i was to fly back to boston early the next morning.
after everyone else had gone to bed, will and i sat
  on the living room couch.

"ann, do you like negligees?"

"i love them, but i never had one . . . i guess it was
  because i honestly never thought i was going to
  have a man. it seemed beyond my wildest
  expectations."

"ann, i am going to start looking for the most
  beautiful negligees around, and i am going to
  buy them for you."
there were tears in his eyes.
he had waited so long to say that to a woman.

the night was late. we were not aware of time or space
  or air or earth . . . only of eternal love . . .
  and matchless designs and sovereign surprises.
we had a sense of galaxies and sonatas and
  deep-flowing rivers in dry, endless deserts . . .
of a God who, if we give Him time, never disappoints
  or lets us down.
the peace transcended every barrier.
a melody played all around us . . . it touched the
  deepest places of our beings.

"honey, this is the first of february.
let's not tell anyone anything until march 1.
let's give God an opportunity, during february,
  to say a resounding 'NO' if we have read
  the signals wrong.

if there are no warnings, on march 1 we will
announce it to the world.''

i was learning to trust will's wisdom and sense of
timing.
and some day, when we have children, i can tell
them their father was a special man . . .
that he was true to his convictions about
intimacy, and didn't yield to his physical
desires . . . until we were married.
my sons will be proud of their father.

from will to ann
february 6, 1981
ann!
i do not know how to love. God is going to teach me
through you what it is to love.

i am not commanding you to do what i am getting ready
to request. it is a concession on your part,
if you so choose.
i would like you to stop eating any foods that have
caffeine ($C_8H_{10}N_4O_2$) in them. i know God has a
time for all of us to go, but we both believe in
cause and effect. you reap what you sow.
if Jesus has given me some knowledge of food, i want you
to know that area, too.
your long-term health is important to me because i love you
and want you with me as i go through life.
but i also want our kids strong and straight . . . without
any possible problems. both caffeine and saccharin
($C_6H_4(CO)(SO_2)NH$) are problem causers. your body is the
biggest influence on our children's formative stages . . .

49

before we can even touch them or see them, you set
the pace.
i even feel the same responsibility about my body, and i
have stopped eating many other things so that if and
when i married and had children, i could tell them
when they grow up that i guarded my eating habits
to give them the best start out of the blocks that i
could.
we need to assume responsibility for our children now.
if we do all we have been given knowledge about,
God will honor and protect the rest.
besides, you would run a better boston without that
stuff. gottcha?

Jesus, teach me to love ann as no woman
has ever been loved before!

will

from ann to will
february 7, 1981
dear will. . .
it seems strange to be writing to you.
i want you to be on the other end of the telephone
where i can hear your voice. . .
or right here in my room, looking at me.

it came to me today, "i bet will is thinking about
a diamond."
let's not think of that right now. it is the last
thing i need. your love, and God's direction. . .
that's what is important.
i love you, not in some squealing, crazy, light-hearted
way. . . but in the most earnest, deep-rooted, tender
sense of totality.

i almost feel shy. . . as if i had NEVER, in any way,
known a man.

i will always remember sitting next to you in the van. . .
and crying. . . crying because it all seemed so amazing
and overwhelming that this man next to me
was going to be my husband. . .
that i was going to leave everything i had ever known
. . . to put my entire life under your authority
and love and care.
as julie would say, "i walked through the vale."

goodnight, my husband-to-be. all my love.

ann

from will to ann
february 9, 1981
ann!
i am so glad that my relationship with you started out
"cold."
it seems that i have a deeper feeling for you each day.
you do not know how important that is for me, because
infatuation would be disastrous.

i need your prayers that i won't think about you all
the time. (fat chance of my getting you to pray
for that.)

in sickness and in health. . .

will

from ann to will
> *february 13, 1981*
> *dear will. . .*

i'm flying home from charlotte, north carolina.
tim and i ran eight miles. . . leg sore, but seems
> *to do better the more i run.*
Jesus says, "ann, you do not need healing. . . or money. . .
> *you need more of ME."*
and i bow my head, embarrassed and ashamed.
"yes, Lord. . . yes. . . yes. . . yes."

i cannot get off my mind your profound, moving
> *statement: "my greatest security in life is*
> *that God really loves me."*
you will never say anything more potent and moving
> *than that.*
when you asked me what was the most secure
> *thing in my life, i did not know exactly how to*
> *answer. when you responded with your statement*
> *about God's love, i was embarrassed, again,*
> *by my shallow place.*

i know, will, that there will be things in each of
> *us that will bug the other at times. . . but to*
> *belong to a man who has so much strength*
> *and individuality. . .*
> *and security. . . and heart for God. . .*
well, i think it will enhance every day of my life.
it will continue to create in me great, wide pools
> *of love and passion for you.*
sometimes i feel a little shaky when i think about
> *camping out, and hiking, and riding rapids. . .*
> *and then i realize, "wow, this is going to be*
> *one whale of an adventure. . . one great, reckless,*

amazing trek through life. . . living with this man.''
i love you, will.
and the feeling of manhood in your letters. . .
in your voice. . . since you have come to love me.
i want to wear beautiful negligees. . . and make
passionate love with you.
i want to listen to your heart. . . to hear your
deepest, most guarded feelings.
i want to reach out in the night and touch your arm,
and know you are there.

i pray that someday i might carry your child, and watch
your face as you love that child and father it.
i pray God might trust us with great causes for His
honor and glory in the world. . . and keep us brave
and singleminded and uncontaminated by the com-
promises of the day. . .
so we can be beacons. . . silently moving down our road. . .
and touching everyone along the way.

i want to have a love relationship with your family.
to enrich their worlds. . . to have hours and hours
to laugh and dream and feel hope.
the plane is landing.
Jesus is our abiding Peace and Joy. . . and you are
my man for life.

love,
ann

from ann to will
february 20, 1981
dear will. . .
my man. . . strong. . . independent. God's.
brave, determined, growing, honest.

a great man . . . my husband-to-be. i love you
    so deeply.
i miss you . . . until i cannot keep the tears from
    finding room in my eyes . . . or stop this quiet little
    pain in my stomach.
every day, i find myself loving you more . . . realizing
    what an incredible, remarkable, amazing
    individualist i am marrying.
realizing what a gift it is that you love me . . . that God
    would allow me this all-encompassing adventure.
grace . . . oh, what grace. i will never be worthy.

moving to idaho falls — to stand at your side in the
    world . . . to start simply . . . to leave a place of
    influence and power and glamor.
oh, will, i am so excited about it. i am so happy.

i have just come from new york city.
knowing chris helps me to know you better.
she is special . . . creative . . . beautiful.
we blend naturally.
she got on an old bike, and rode by me as I ran my miles
    through central park . . . telling me all about your
    heritage . . . three and four generations back.
then we found an old man who said he would watch
    the bike if we paid him. we did, so we could
    go in (running clothes and all) to bonwit's
    and look at wedding dresses. just for fun.

she gives the credit for her being a great artist
    to your mom, saying your mother put big fat
    crayons in her hand when she was three.
i hope your mother will do that with our children, too.

i am committed to you, will . . . forever . . . totally . . .
   with joy.

i am home again from another road trip.
boston . . . this city of culture and magic. this city
   that has won my heart and captivated my whole
   inner pool of creativity . . . until you came.
we will start our lives here . . . and then i will —
   quietly, with peace — leave a part of me here.
and "whither thou goest, i will go . . .
   thy people shall be my people . . . my life. . . ."
goodnight, my hero . . . my partner . . . my lover . . . my man.

                                                  ann

february 1981

without telling me, will called my parents in
   late february.
"this is will anderson. i am a thirty-seven-year-old
   potato farmer from idaho and i'm in love with
   your daughter. i feel God is calling me to marry her.
   could i fly down for the weekend?"

"well, oh, my . . . uh . . . yes . . . what was your name?
does ann know about these plans?"

he bounded off the plane in san francisco . . . ten
   pounds of potatoes in a mesh bag in one hand,
   a briefcase in the other.
seeing a rather small, gray-haired man who looked as
   if he might be my father, he picked harold kiemel
   up and whirled him around.
he walked out to the curb, eyed my mother at the car,
   and did the same thing to her.
mom said she liked him the first instant she caught

my husband, william earle anderson, II,
on the ranch.

sight of him. he was full of energy and vitality
and strength.

the next weekend, he called my brother in san
bernardino, california.
"fred, my name is will anderson. i'm in love with
your sister . . . and being the older brother to two
sisters, i know that big brothers have a special
role in every family. may i come to see you
and marlene?"

he carried tasha, two years old, around. took long
walks with fred around the mountain roads where
they live in running springs. talked to marlene
about babies and breast-feeding.

finally it was time to go to cleveland to meet
jan and tom. he felt the whole family should
give their approval or our marriage should not be.
jan was apprehensive. who was this man?
of all the people, her stamp of approval was most
important because she knew me better than *anyone*.
they hired a baby-sitter for the little boys,
and took will out to dinner.
immediately there was approval and rapport.

"tom and jan, before i met ann, i had a whole list of
absolutes for whoever was to be my wife.
she had to have a certain figure, a certain
background . . . well, a lot of specifications.
i had waited a long time. then i met ann.
i realized this was God's woman for me . . . his perfect
program.
she was too skinny. she was not exactly what i had
in mind, but suddenly it did not matter.

who was i to question God about the woman He had
   spent thirty-five years getting ready for me . . .
   thirty-five years of preparation?
even if she were to get multiple sclerosis or cancer
   tomorrow, i am going to marry her on june 7.
i am committed to her as long as we both live.''

something happens between a man and a woman . . .
   a friend and a friend. . . .
   the Savior and a person . . . when this level
   of commitment is reached.
the Divine overtakes the human . . . the eternal the
   temporal.
though will anderson should lose both his legs . . .
   or say we are moving to cuba to grow potatoes
   the rest of our lives,
i am his wife until death.

from julie to ann
   february 21, 1981
   dearest ann . . .
*i jogged down the road to the mailbox, and there
   was your letter.*
*after reading it, i went to a special place
   by the creek that flows through our property
   and i knelt down and thanked our Lord Jesus
   with my whole heart.*
*i knelt there by the creek with the sound of bubbling,
   dancing water flowing through the meadow,
   and i wept and wept tears of JOY.*
i kept telling Jesus, ''i'm so happy.''

yes, ann, we will be family . . . blood . . . and we and

my husband and my mother-in-law, before a roaring fire
at the home place. i feel so loved.

our children will dream together in Jesus.
there will be wonderful times together as family
  in front of happy fireplaces and by dancing
  mountain streams.
God's grace and love and mercy will surround us and
  follow us all the days of our lives.

in Jesus' great love,

                            julie and tom

from will to ann
  february 22, 1981
  dearest ann...
i know we will be able to face any problem because i
  am totally committed to you.
with commitment comes a calm assurance that everything
  can be handled.
remember that LOVE never fails because it is primarily
  a commitment, not a feeling.
i am so comfortable with you. as far as i am concerned,
  you never have to change, one iota.
i like you just the way you are put together.
i know you are going to be my best advisor in talking
  about my business. Jesus is going to give you
  insights into aspects of this area that i would
  never have seen before.
your loving husband!

                                   will

from will to ann
  february 23, 1981
  ann, i hope i can experience and feel what you do for

*me forever . . . but most of all, i want to make you
    happy.
we have such a short time on this earth, and i want to
    spend the rest of my life making you happy.
    (smother! smother! smother!)*

*i hope you enjoy praying. a praying wife is such a
    strong link in the chain. i feel that behind
    every successful Christian is a prayer warrior,
    so pray for me.
looking forward to june 7 . . .*

                                                    will

from will to ann
    february 24, 1981
        ann . . .
*you cannot understand the volcanic emotions that are
    flowing to the surface in will anderson.
all these years of being cool, calm, and collected . . .
all these years of staying "arm's length" from emotional
    involvement . . .
all these years of praying for a woman of God that He
    was preparing just for me!
ann, i am your bond servant for life.
a bond servant was a man who freely submitted himself to
    another as a servant for life because he loved and
    wanted to spend the rest of his life serving the
    other person.
i pledge myself to you as your bond servant, as a vow
    before God and man.*

                                                    will

from elisabeth elliot gren to ann
february 24, 1981
dearest ann. . .
i wanted to write to assure you of my love and prayers
for you, and especially of my huge delight that
you are to be married!
it's simply wonderful, and i do thank God for this almost
unhoped-for answer to my prayers for you.
i had been committing you to God for His whole will to
be accomplished in and through you, and trusting Him
to answer as He saw fit, but this is the "exceeding
abundantly above. . . ."

God finally (after five and a half years of silence and
uncertainty and waiting while i loved him) gave me
jim. little did i imagine, of course, that he would
be given for only twenty-seven months. . . but again,
i know that my loving Lord's loving-kindness will
ultimately be shown, even in that.

ann, we all have problems with the way people come across.
lars gets on me for coming across as silent and
hostile and sometimes rude to one or two people who
are close to me.
i have gotten onto you for coming across as egotistical,
for not using enough Scripture in your messages,
for drawing attention to the things you do for Jesus.
but i see in you a heart hungry for God, for all He wants
to give you and to make of you, and who can ask more
of any Christian?
each of us has his blind spots. each of us is at a
different stage of his pilgrimage. we are
simply toiling up a very steep hill with a crooked
stick, our faces toward the Celestial City, all

of us wholly and utterly dependent on that grace
that is greater than all our sin.

i thank God for you and for bringing us together.
how i'd love to meet will.
God bless you and keep you and make His face shine on you.
much love,

elisabeth

march 1981

how to get from march 1 to june 7...the date we
    had set for the wedding?
how could i tie all the ends together...phase out
    this part of my life? it all seemed monumental.
my whole world had centered in boston...my
    neighborhood...the children...the
    gymnasium...
    my condominium...and offices.
how could i leave this city that held my heart in its
    hands...where i had poured out so much energy
    and love...where all my dreams had centered?

Jesus knew. His plan is so uncomplicated...the
    pieces in His program are so clean and simple
    and easily executed if we are waiting...
    listening...for the clues.

there was mollie cox, my bookkeeper. she came from
    my very own neighborhood...i had helped her
    find Jesus several years before.
when she heard i was getting married, she realized she
    would be free to join her daughter, cynthia, in
    los angeles. several months before, the Lord had
    shifted cynthia from new york to the west coast...

preparing the new way, the new place.

mollie was one of my real neighborhood miracles . . .
my shining star in a cold corner. mollie . . . with
british accent and fast stride and wonderful
cooking.

i could never have left mollie hanging, without a
job . . . i was committed to her for life.

but in february she had moved west to be with
cynthia.

andie goodrich, my secretary, was scheduled to leave
on june 1 . . . her husband, craig, was graduating
from law school and had accepted a position in
washington, d.c.

it was andie who had insisted i not let will anderson
leave town without meeting him. . . .

there never could have been a wedding without andie,
and God kept her there 'til the last moment
i needed her.

it was very hard to say goodbye to andie, too. i loved
her so much. but it was the right time for us
both . . . obedience isn't based on emotion, but is
an act of the will.

every day i was learning more about that.

tim woodbridge, my newest road man, had been with
me for a year and had run four marathons with me.

he was getting his master's degree in business and was
taking a position on the faculty of eastern nazarene
college . . . would also be married on august 1.

i would need a new person to travel with me, anyway.

tying the ends . . . bringing closure . . . showing me the
"yeses" so i would not be afraid . . .
so i would know this was GOD'S.

rays of bright morning sun . . . traces of mercy and
   gentle smoothing of my divided heart: so loving
   will . . . so tied to boston.

then there was my apartment . . . on the wharf . . .
   the salty atlantic lapping at the dock below
   my window . . . the sound of fog horns on misty
   nights . . . ocean liners tooting . . . and seagulls.
the noises of the city . . . the church chimes.
all of boston's skyline across the window — so i could
   lie in bed and trace the pointed roofs . . . and the
   flat ones . . . and pray for all the people behind
   the stone walls and the windows.
i just couldn't sell this little studio sanctuary that
   had protected me from crowds and fears and harm
   during difficult times. these walls that had watched
   both poor people and rich kneel by the couch and
   pray and believe.
my small kitchen where i had baked so many cookies
   and fixed popcorn for my neighborhood people.
this building was almost two hundred years
   old . . . and magnificent.
surely Jesus would want me just to rent it, but keep it
   as my own . . . perhaps will and i could vacation
   there sometimes in summer when our schedules
   allowed.
"ann," will said, "it's your decision. if you want to
   keep 430 lewis wharf, you can. i'll pray you will
   know the right thing to do."
no pressure . . . no crowding . . . no ultimatums.
he always, then and now, has given me freedom,
   knowing God guards and guides my heart.

as i knelt by my bed one night, it came to me that
   i must let go . . . that i was no longer going to

be the same woman with the same mission.
there would be a wider mission . . . a new place.
when abraham followed God, he left everything —
    ALL — with no questions or clinging
    sentiment . . . not even knowing exactly where
    it would lead.
God's desire was that i not cling to the past . . . or
    try to hang on . . . or refuse to let go of an emotional
    attachment.
will was my man . . . i was going to him, leaving all.
    counting home and familiar things and human
    securities as nothing to follow the Quiet Voice.
    my real Leader. to take God's hand and allow
    Him to lead me to my husband . . . and to my fresh,
    new place.

two days after i put my little studio condominium on
    the market, it was sold for more than twice
    the amount i had paid for it.
as i took the pictures off the walls . . . and pulled the
    dishes out of the cupboards . . . and rolled up
    the bedspread . . . there were some tears.
a tendency to pull back . . . to say, "i *can't.*"
    to be overwhelmed and afraid.
then i would straighten up . . . shake off the trembling,
    tempting thoughts . . . and my face would break
    into a smile.
and i'd hear a song outside the window pane.

o God of stars and flowers, forgive our blindness,
no dream of night hath dared what Thou hast wrought . . .
new every morning is Thy loving-kindness . . .
far, far above what we had asked or thought.

(amy carmichael)

from will to ann
  march 10, 1981
  dearest ann anderson!
i cannot believe i have these feelings of needing you.
it is not just a physical "grab-grab"... but just to
    have you in the same house... to talk... to look at you.
i have never felt this way about anyone. ME?
    need anyone? NEVER, in a hundred, never in a
    thousand, never in a million years!
(the bigger they are, the harder they fall. that's me.)

miss you more and more each day.

                                                    will

from ann to will
  march 11, 1981
  dear will,
every day i feel this quiet, rich joy that you are
    soon (but not soon enough) to be my husband.
that it is so much more than romance... than sheer
  intrigue... or some passing infatuation.
that i will literally become totally one with you.
    forever. ordained by God.
i am so glad.

                                                    ann

from ann to will
  march 12, 1981
  dear will...
i read something today by eugenia price... it touched
    me deeply:
"the only direct statement of Jesus that is simple enough

for me to comprehend when my heart is breaking or
when i am discouraged or scared is: 'FOLLOW ME'. . .
i cannot understand life because life is not understandable, but i can grasp, 'FOLLOW ME'. . . . ''

honey, along the road you and i will have places that
will be very difficult. . . and confusing. . .
NOT understandable from human perspective.
i pray we never forget, simply, to "follow."

i want to share my whole life with you. and more than
that, i want us to share our every tomorrow with our
Creator and Savior. . . and thus, the world.
at any cost.
tonight i run my hand across your shoulders. . .
and breathe into your heart.
tonight i thank God for you.

ann

from will to ann
march 18, 1981
ann. . .
i want to be used in the lives of other people, but
you are my most important neighbor.
("Jesus, teach me what it means to 'love my neighbor
as myself.' ")
if i never meet the needs of another individual other
than you, that could be success for me.
i do pray to be used by Jesus in all areas of my life,
but i so desire that you will be built up by our
relationship and love.

you are like a small seed planted in my heart.

*i can feel the roots reaching into my spirit, gaining a firm
    grip on my being, and as that is happening, i am
    experiencing emotions and feelings that have never
    passed my way before.*
Jesus has used you as an answer to make me complete.
as you say, "Jesus loves me, this i know!"
and i say to you, "will loves you, this i know!"

> *will*

from will to ann
    march 26, 1981
    ann!
*we grow BIG potatoes in idaho, and potato growers
    have BIG hearts. . . and mine is all yours!*
i love you a whole train load!

> *will*

from will to ann
    april 4, 1981
    ann. . .
*woman, you fill me up like a river fills its bed in
    spring.*
*the water rises and overflows. . . spreads out and
    people find it impossible to keep it in control.*
that is how i feel about you.
*love keeps growing and spreading into all aspects
    of my heart and soul and life.*
God's love does the same. . . nobody can contain it!
love forever,

> *me*

from will to ann
> *april 12, 1981*
> *dear ann. . .*

if you came down with polio or multiple sclerosis;
> *if they had to carry you to the front of the church*
> *on a stretcher. . .*

i am marrying you.
your man,

> > > > > > > > > > *will*

from ann to will
> *april 14, 1981*
> *dear beloved husband (for though i have never slept*
> *with you, or gone down a church aisle, yet. . .*
> *i am already committed to you).*

i feel so emotional — like i want to cry and cry.
> *i do not even know exactly why. . .*
> *frustrated because you are so far away.*
> *angry because we share so little, and when we are*
> *together, it is abnormal. . . racing. . . racing.*

no walks in the country. nothing laid back.
> *just hectic and pressured, like the rest of the world.*

oh, honey, will our lives ever be normal?

i miss experiencing *you. there are always so many*
> *people. too many major decisions.*

i hope marriage is not going to be a huge adjustment
> *for us. traumatizing. i do not want it to be.*

i feel so emotional about the marathon, too.

in my mind, it seems so possible. . . and then i get out
> *to run, and i feel the pain.*

yet i think of jock's love for me. . . and that it might
> *be my last boston for awhile.*

well, Jesus is my only Hope. He knows ALL about injuries.

you are always "gentle on my mind. ..."

ann

from gloria gaither to ann
    april 16, 1981
    dear ann,
bill and i are very happy for you. marriage is the
    greatest way to go!
i wish you an amy, a benjy, and a suzanne.
i wish you starry nights, and candles burning, and walks
    in the fields.
i wish you dairy queens and hot beaches.
i wish you quiet suppers, and fires in the fireplace,
    and regular days.
i wish you plenty of time to argue and get things
    cleared out.
i wish you problems to solve together, obstacles to
    climb together, fears to conquer together.
i wish you freedom from suspicion but not freedom from
    mystery.
may you NEVER learn all there is to know about each other.
i wish you growth and change.
you are loved!

gloria

april 1981

the time for the boston marathon was drawing
    near...
once again thousands of spectators would be crowding
    around the 26.2-mile course.

but would i be able to run?

on my winter trip to israel, three months before,
    as i had run the israeli marathon a second time,
    i had torn a muscle on the fifteenth mile.
though i was able, in spite of great pain. . .and
    through tears. . .to finish, it had left me
    severely injured for the months preceding the
    boston.

during those three months, wherever i traveled, i
    went to the exercise room to work with weights. . .
    to make my body stronger, though i could hardly
    run.
not once did i run without some pain. often i could
    do only twenty or twenty-five miles a week.
the marathon began to look more and more
    impossible, but i refused to be deterred.
faithfulness. . .that's what paid.
that is what Jesus cares about.
if i did all i possibly could, and then was unable to
    run, at least i would have peace of mind, knowing
    i had given my very best.

"oh, Jesus, you have so blessed me. . .
You allowed me to run six marathons my first year
    of running. . .but i SO want to run the boston
    this year. . . .
it may be my last. i'm leaving the boston area. . .
    and. . .oh, Jesus, please."
(The Lord must have become weary of my whining
    and tears over injuries in my running. He
    certainly used them to mellow me and break
    me, and teach me his power and strength.)

three days before the marathon, will decided to
    come east. though he knew i might not be running,
    he thought he should be there, just in case . . . to
    cheer me on . . . to scream at the sidelines.
he knew i would need miracles to get me through the
    long, grueling boston course.

the night before, i crawled into bed with a quiet,
    yielded heart.
"Jesus, i'll pin my number on and go as far as i can.
i will be happy WHATEVER you choose . . . only You
    can see me through this.
if at mile eight i have pain, i will drop out and
    trust Your sovereign plan.
Jesus, i have begged and pleaded and worried . . . that
    is sin.
now i surrender to you."

april 20 was overcast . . . in the forties . . . some
    drizzling rain. perfect weather for the long run.
with tears in my eyes, i pinned my number on . . .
    gooped vaseline all over my toes . . . pulled on
    old shorts and a special tee-shirt jock semple
    had given me to wear, to show i was a member of the
    boston athletic association.
when the gun went off, cindy smith was at my side.
her enthusiasm was amazing. she was healthy, strong,
    excited, ready.
"cindy, don't let me slow you down. when you feel
    like moving out, you go right ahead.
i probably can only run a few miles.
i'm praying for you, cindy. atta girl! *you can do it!*"

the gun went off and we started running. there were
    thousands of runners . . . balloons . . . bands

playing . . . screaming crowds. we heard coughs and
some heavy breathing as we all tried to find our
right pace and move past the first mile.
i was very cautious, thinking that if i ran an eight-
minute mile, i could go farther.
maybe, if i could survive until the eighteenth mile . . .
and heartbreak hill . . . i could walk some of the five
miles of hills.
but it was in God's hands . . . total relaxation . . . no
stress . . . no fear as i moved into my pace.
suddenly i began to notice cindy lagging behind.
it shocked me . . . was i actually feeling *good?*
cindy yelled, "ann, keep going. you look strong.
this is your day. i'm praying for *you.*"

picking up my pace, i began to move out . . . wearing
a huge smile . . . reaching out to pat all the
children's heads along the sidelines, or grab
their hands, screaming, "God loves you . . . God
bless you . . . ."
i sang my little songs to the other runners. i
watched every face i passed. my eyes were
brimming with the love i felt for them.
this was my world . . . my town . . . my turf.
i had loved these crowds, prayed for them, desired
new life for them.
this was my farewell.

though they could not hear the words,
in my heart i was telling them i had loved
them from afar and was now leaving them . . .
but not leaving them alone.
there was a Comforter . . . a Savior.
and others would come to boston with like vision

and open heart to take my place. to laugh
and cry with them.

at the heartbreak hills, i actually passed runners.
not once did i even stop for a drink, but would
   now and then grab a cup of water held out to
   me by a child . . . take a few swallows while still
   in motion . . . then throw the cup down and go on.
turning the last corner, i could finally see the
   finish line three hundred yards ahead.
the crowds were so immense and the din of the cheers
   so intense and incredible, that i felt my entire
   being, lifted . . . carried . . . and gracefully lured to
   the finish.
never once had i looked at a clock or considered my
   speed. all along the way i had said, ''Jesus,
   if you want me to stop at any mile, i will.
   Thy will be done.''
until the final mile, i was not sure whether Jesus
   would allow me to cover the entire course.

as i came across the finish, i looked up at the clock.
not only had i finished, i had run fast enough to
   automatically requalify me for next year's
   marathon.

it was a crown of blessing . . . a final farewell.
a perfect closure to this grand and magnificent era
   in my life.
suddenly, down under the prudential building,
   among the weary runners, i heard a child's voice:
   ''ann kiemel! ann kiemel! YOU DO IT AGAIN!''
i could scarcely believe my eyes . . . it was eleven-
   year-old pablo, a child i had taken to israel
   more than a year before.

pablo — a small dreamer in a cold, hard world.
"ann kiemel, today is my birthday. i run all the
way from my housing project. i run to see you
do it again.
oh, ann kiemel, you and Jesus. . .you do it again!"

tears. . .hugs. . .broken spanish words melting into
my tired heart.
one small boy at the end of one giant dream. . .
to remind me he will still be there to carry
the love of Jesus, our Savior.
to take my place as i head for idaho.
alleluia. alleluia. amen.

from bob benson to ann
april 20, 1981
dear ann. . .
the other evening when i got home, peg said,
"sit down, i want to read something very, very nice."
and with her brown eyes moist with happiness for you,
she read your letter to me. we are both very
happy for you and will.
we want to come to idaho sometimes and see the school
teacher, dean, writer, speaker, runner, and
now potato farmer.
God bless.

bob

from will to ann
april 26, 1981
dearest honey. . .
i cannot believe you have never camped out in your life.
you must have been kidding???

someone with your wide background. . . never camping?
alas, alack, poor ann.
but hark! see rugged idaho woodsman yonder.
will he save the day? hooray! yes.
he will lead the way for the cute little city woman.

well, Lord, you have given me the desire of my heart
in this woman. i wonder if she will fit into your
beautiful woods? (if i know my ann, she will love it.)
me

from chrisi to ann
   april 29, 1981
   dear ann,
my new sister-in-law. . . i'm ecstatic, and can
   hardly wait.
your love for one another would transform a potato
   patch into a magnificent flower-filled cathedral
   with falling stars for candles and angels for the
   music!
He has all under His wings. i love you.
your kid sister,
                              chrisi
p.s. congrats on the b. marathon!

from ann to will
   may 3, 1981
   dear will. . .
could you please buy some new white tee shirts?
   and some knee-length socks?

honey, i keep praying about your clothes. . .

and about letting you be you. accepting you
   as you are.
i have always wanted instant change. i am such a
   perfectionist. . . and loving you (which i do,
   fiercely and with fervor) has shown up more of
   my flaws than anything.
i find myself wanting you to be certain ways. . . it does
   not mean it is necessarily right.
sometimes i am frightened over marriage. i keep running
   toward the goal, concentrating all my energies on
   faith in God's love to give me what i need, to be
   your woman. to make you deeply happy.
i know God is wanting to change all the shallow things
   in me. please pray for me!

                                                   ann

from dr. kenneth taylor to ann
   may 7, 1981
   hi, ann. . .
*yes, since i pray for you in private
   i will be glad to do the same in
   public. . . at your wedding.*
blessings,

                              ken taylor

from will to ann
   may 7, 1981
   ann!
*well, i never thought we would be down to thirty
   days. one month and i will be waiting for you
   up front.*
i love the verses:

let your manhood be a blessing; rejoice in the wife
of your youth. let her charms and tender embraces
satisfy you. let her love alone fill you with
delight.

ann, my goal as a husband is as follows:
   "a great lover is someone who can satisfy one woman
   all her life long. . . and who can be satisfied by one
   woman all his life long. a great lover is not someone
   who goes from woman to woman. any dog can do that."
i don't need conquests to establish my identity or
   macho needs.
ann, i want you to understand how much i admire and love
   you for the load you are carrying for the wedding.
there is so much to do. . . so many details. . . so much
   pressure.
woman, i respect you more than any woman in the world.
you are truly a thoroughbred! love,
                                          will

from ann to will
   may 8, 1981
   good morning, darling. . .
now we start saying it is less than a month
   until we will be ONE. . . when we will
   lie side-by-side. . . and awaken to each
   other's presence.
sharing all our joys. . . and tests. . . and sorrows.
together.
have a beautiful, rich day!
                                          ann

happy belonging under wide idaho sky.

from will to ann
  may 15, 1981
  ann!
did i ever tell you that after the baptism
  service at the sea of galilee,
i hopped a bus to visit a kibbutz in northwest israel?

you had me confused,
our relationship was totally platonic.
i had not even held your hand, yet i was feeling
  emotions that i had never felt before.
i was not able to articulate to myself or anyone else
  what was happening inside.

you were nice and had touched me in a unique way,
  but you did not fit any of the items on
  my "list."
as the bus was traveling through nazareth, i felt
  as if there was a big steel egg in my gut
  and that God was peeling the shell.
inside was this ball of compassion, emotion,
  tenderness, and love for you.
it was such a physical response, i felt sick.
i leaned my head weakly on the window and looked out
  at a dirty, dingy town that had not changed in
  two thousand years.
i remembered what the pharisees had said:
  "can any good thing come out of nazareth?"

and i knew that the answer was twice wrong.
                              love, will

from ann to will
   may 24, 1981
   darling...
two weeks from today... our wedding.
this is the way i used to count off days before a
   marathon... trembling... expectant... scared.
commiting my entire being to you... forever...
   taking on not only what life holds for me,
   but whatever God and life bring your way...
what an amazing place for two independent people!

oh, honey... i am really ready to become your wife.
today was my last public appearance as ann kiemel,
   single woman.
i never thought this moment would come.
i am most amazed by the progression of events...
   feelings... attitudes... i actually feel a part of you.
you are not a foreign entity that i am walking toward.
you are not just a person i look at... love and admire
   and respect from a distance.
you are now truly a part of me. you have become
   vulnerable with me. opened your heart to me.
   touched the innermost part of me.
i am no longer afraid.

will, i love the story of your name... of your dad
   deciding that "bill" was not adequate.
   it was like the bill of a duck, or something
   that needed to be paid...
but "will" represented the courage to make it.
   through anything... never to give up...
   to pull out anything and everything from inside
   you to get the job done.
the thought of your dad's, too, about being the best
   at what you do — i liked that.

if you are a ditch-digger, then be the best one,
*   and someday you will dig the panama canal.*
or, with potatoes, take the job to heart. do not
*   switch from job to job; become the number-one*
*   potato farmer in the world. solid philosophy!*

i love what i feel when i am next to you.
how you taste when we kiss.
how you think.
i care so much about what you feel.
you and jan will always be my best friends . . .
*   each in a different dimension . . . BUT*
my total life belongs only to Jesus and you.

in my mind, i keep seeing your hermiston crop.
*   watching you and darrell and randy unload that*
*   heavy machinery . . . march with authority through*
*   the rows of potatoes.*
i have decided that a man of the earth can make it through
*   anything . . . if some day, we are stranded on the other side*
*   of the world with no one . . . and no money . . . you will*
*   be able to take care of me.*

you are my man. thank you for loving me.
that, in itself, will touch the world.

ann

from elisabeth elliot gren to ann
    june 1, 1981
    dear ann . . .
i am convinced satan's primary target to destroy
*   the church and the country is the Christian*
*   family.*

stand strong, ann. love will.
be respectful, obedient, gentle. . .
   and as soon as any single thought occurs
   to you that is not obedient to Christ,
   bring it into "captivity" before it becomes
   a stronghold.
a thought turns into a consideration, which becomes
   an attitude, then action, then habit,
   then stronghold!
let God be the stronghold of your life. ps. 27:1
love you much, ann.

                          elisabeth

june 7, 1981

today in park street church, downtown boston,
i married william earle anderson II.

when i was very small, my father had said,
   "Jesus pays."

I replied, "how does He pay, daddy?
   i am eight years old and ugly,
   and hardly anyone likes me."

   "give God time. you'll see."

for thirty-five years i had walked and run and
   stumbled and limped. laughed and screamed
   and felt wonder and cried.
sometimes the days seemed eternal, and the sky dark.

ten years ago, thousands of miles away, on his

father's potato ranch, a young man had prayed,
"Father God, give me a woman of God.
a woman committed to you.
someone strong where i am weak.
make me the man she needs. build her . . . guide
her . . . prepare her . . . bless her."
reckless and independent and strong.
trained by his genius father. adored by his younger
sisters. educated, at times, overseas.
at home with mountains and fishing and animals and
nesting eagles.
a straight arrow. no-nonsense.
unafraid of almost everything. God's.

will had waited. i had waited.
God had spared my whole family to join in the
celebration.

luncheons had been given in my honor . . .
by elva ruth wylie, of dallas, at the harvard club.
by dot mccollister, of baton rouge, at the
ritz-carlton.
a reception by the head of ceremonies, paul miller,
in washington, d.c.
a reception by the fishers in pennsylvania.
four showers.
words of advice and music and love and
beautifully wrapped presents.
tears . . . always tears and amazement that this love
could really be showered on me.

there was a private dinner for family at the berry's.
we all received an incredible surprise when my
brother, fred, and his wife, marlene, with two-year
old tasha and nineteen-day-old sean paul, appeared.

it was everyone's first glimpse of the only boy child to
   carry the kiemel name.
another dinner for closest, out-of-town friends at the
   copley hotel . . . with baked potatoes brought by
   will from idaho . . . fresh seafood.
   an intimate time when friends tossed out stories
   about will and me.
   james hetherington and ron ziegler were masters
   of ceremonies.

on our wedding day i took a twelve-mile run
   at dawn to bid my last good-bye to
   the charles river and a beloved city.
it was pentecost sunday . . . shining sky . . .
   summer breeze . . . low 70's . . . radiant sun.
   and the Holy Spirit's presence.

will's college football hero, and one of my
   favorite Christians, raymond berry,
   took me down the aisle.
my father married will and me, assisted by dr. paul
   toms, pastor of park street church, and
   dr. ken taylor, paraphraser of *The Living Bible*.
   clark peddicord, who works with campus crusade
   in germany, prayed.
children from my gymnasium project sang. they
   wore choir robes and carried fresh flowers.
   as they followed steve, the guitarist, people
   cheered . . . cried.

jo anne ferguson and sally berry directed everything.
   there were fifty pots of gloxinia — all colors —
   on all the winding steps leading to the sanctuary.
   more potted plants and palms and twenty

i really was a bride. i really had a wedding
dress. . .imported french lace.
it's still like a dream.

candelabra across the front of the church...
hurricane candles on every pew...roses and
baby's breath.

my wedding gown was made entirely of heavy white
    imported french lace. i wore an exquisite veil of
    imported lace, loaned to me by andie, my secretary,
    who had worn it in her wedding.
the men were in gray tails...ten of them, plus will.
my only attendant was jan, my sister...my favorite
    person. she wore navy taffeta and organdy, with
    a wide hot-pink sash...all sewn by my mother.

tre, four years old...jan's son...my firstborn
    nephew and child of my heart...holding his
    mother's hand, carried a rose and will's
    wedding band.
("mom, i have to go potty."
    eyes pleading...legs crossed.
    all those people. one small boy.
    one great panic. but he made it.)

will's beautiful sisters, julie and chrisi,
    lit the candles.

people from twenty-eight states and germany came.
    the very rich. the very poor.
    all racial backgrounds.
    those with faith. those without.
    side by side.
joe and patti catalana, just in from a race in alaska.
jock semple in the third row.
the builder of the gymnasium, with his three
    grown sons and their wives.
maintenance men from my building.

at the wedding, with my nephews, tre and nash.

randy, who worked in will's potato harvest in oregon,
    hitchhiked across the country to be there...
    eyes shining with tears.

there were dozens of bright pink, helium-filled
    balloons for all the children as they came
    out of the church...balloons that climbed the
    sky, floated over church steeples and trees
    and crowded old buildings...capturing hundreds
    of eyes and hearts. calling them to celebrate
    too.

a horse-drawn carriage took will and me for a ride
    around boston common, then to the parker
    house hotel for the reception.
(it was at the parker house where i had first met will.)
    along the way people cheered and hailed the
    unknown bride and groom.
there was a large, many-tiered cake to serve
    hundreds...and a fruit punch.
no receiving line...but people waited to speak to us,
    and for three and a half hours, will and i
    hugged and cried and visited and celebrated with
    every single guest.
the photographer was hard at work.
i let a little friend...an eleven-year-old spanish
    girl...wear my veil.
    i kissed children's faces.
they had tears in their eyes as we parted...
    joy mixed with sadness as i bade farewell
    to so many i had loved and prayed over
    in that grand old city for so long.
some had come in wheelchairs. some children, racked
    by serious disease, had come from faraway places
    and waited for hours...because they loved me.

a girl from a midwestern university,
two sisters from warroad, minnesota.
the biggest buyer of will's organically grown
potatoes, sal cipriano, of boston — also his
partner from new york city, tom devine.
big hands. smooth, cameoed faces.

in the church, at the close of the ceremony,
as my father pronounced us husband and wife,
the congregation broke out in spontaneous
applause...on and on. then they rose from
their places, tears streaming...faces radiant.
a standing ovation.
we will never forget...and will wear their joy
in our hearts forever.
oh, daddy, daddy, you were right when you told me,
long years ago,
"Jesus changes everything...*everything*...
in His time."

our wedding vows...june 7, 1981
ann kiemel, i stand before these friends today
with joy in my heart as i receive you as my wife.

i have seen many specific prayers answered in the
last few years, but never have i felt God's
direction in my life as i have in the events leading
up to this day.

i love you. i cherish you. i honor you.
i am committed to you. i have prayed for you.
i've waited for you. you are my woman.

as Jesus loves me unconditionally, i give you

my life and unconditional love.

as a ring has no end, i give you this token
  of my love for you and my commitment to you
  for as long as we both shall live.

will anderson, i love you.
i accept this ring with so much joy.
you are my husband, my man. today, i come into your
  life to become one with you.
of all the men in the world, you are God's perfect
  choice for me.

i want to laugh and cry with you. to dream with you.
to be unafraid with you. to climb mountains with you.
to love and cherish you. to be faithful.

i submit to you, my husband. . . as unto the Lord,
  even if some call it old-fashioned.
it is Jesus, my Savior, who will give me strength
  and power to live out these vows.

i also give you a ring. . . as a symbol of our union. . .
  and of my devotion to you as long as we both live.

each of us had a Scripture verse engraved in the
  other's wedding band.
i gave will proverbs 3:5 and 6 —
  trust in the Lord with all thine heart;
  and lean not unto thine own understanding.
  in all thy ways acknowledge Him,
  and He shall direct thy paths.

92

will gave me romans 8:28:
and we know that God causes all things to
work together for good to those who love God,
to those who are called according to His purpose.

from harold kiemel to will
september 8, 1981
dear will. . .
i love you, my own will. my own precious son-in-law!
remember. . . when you are out in the potato fields,
i am with you. . . with faith in God and you.
i thank God for your skill and knowledge. . .
most of all i will pray that our Lord Jesus
shall give you His Holy Spirit in grace and
wisdom and power to inspire, comfort, encourage,
and bless you and ann forever in His holy service!
thank you for being a good husband to ann.
she loves you and so do we!
love and prayers.
                                        h.k.
p.s. please pray for us that we shall lift up our
Lord Jesus and be a blessing for Him.

september 1981

recently i received this letter from a young woman
    somewhere in the united states:
dear ann, i feel so worthless when i think of you.
in my heart i think you matter a thousand times more
to the Father than i do. . . that you are worth blessing;
i am not.
i believe God favors you. . . shields you from hurt and
anguish. . . gives you everything.
i am insignificant to God.

*God's blessing upon you is so obvious. . . He has rubber-
    stamped His love all over you.*
*i cannot see His working in my life, let alone
    His blessing.*
*i think it is pretty easy for you to be chipper and
    to chant your little motto: "serving Jesus pays. . . ."*
*ann, ever since i learned of your marriage, i have been
    living under a cloud of depression.*
you were a comfort and model for me as a single woman.
now i feel resentment to God for blessing you in every way.
i want to be happy for you, but my attitude is lousy.
next to you, i feel worthless.
*do you have it all, ann? is your life squeaky clean
    with excitement? do you want for anything?
    do you struggle?*

illusions. believing that someone else's place or
    possession is more important or better than
    whatever is mine.
before i married will anderson, on one bleak,
    drizzling morning in idaho falls, we went
    out for a run. . .just a few miles.
i had been visiting him between speaking dates, and
    was flying on later that morning.

"ann, it is easy for people to be led astray by
    illusions."
his voice was sober. deep.
i glanced over and noticed that his face was strangely
    fixed. jaw very square. a line across his brow.
    his eyes blacker than ever before. penetrating.
"the only way we will both be contented throughout
    life and always really love each other is to
    remember that an illusion is the devil's greatest
    tool to destroy us.

years down the road, when i am out of town on
  business and see a sexy woman with a lot of
  moves. . . and you are far away. . . i must
  remember that what she offers is an illusion. . .
  that what she has is not better than what God
  gave me in you. and vice versa.''

the rain was making tiny tickling streams down my
  face and neck. clouds were hanging low over the
  distant mountain peaks.
it was a country road. no airplanes in the distance,
  or cars or motorcycles or people.
    quiet earth. still, quiet heart.
this was God's chosen man for me. . . for as long as we
  both lived.
he was speaking a truth that i had come to understand
  well.
to be unhappy in God's plan for us is a sin.
to wish i were married instead of single. . . single
  rather than married.
that my husband looked like someone else's husband,
  or had a better, more prestigious job like another
  man. to wish i had a house like mary's, or that we
  drove a car like john's. . .
    and actually to be unhappy about it is rejecting
    God's will for me right now in my life.
to be emotionally crippled because the other women
  have babies, and i do not. . . or furs and
  diamonds.
to cling to illusions. . . to believe them. . .
    to compare our lives. . . to find the grass greener
    somewhere else.
it is sin.
it spoils God's creativity in me where i am now.
it minimizes everything He could do for me.

no one . . . absolutely *no one* . . . has everything.

anyone who has accomplished something significant
in life has done so with sacrifice and pain.

often, children who turn out to be prominent and
successful come from homes where the parents
have never had much materially, but have been
faithful, hard workers all their lives.

God rewards them through their children.

likewise, wealthy corporate executives, with huge
expense accounts and fancy, columned homes on
winding drives, may have a very sick wife . . . or a
cold loveless marriage . . . or a child on drugs,
indifferent to the parents' hard work and
sacrifice.

people who take evening drives through elegant
neighborhoods to "ooh" and "ahh" over
impressive mansions, wonder what it must be
like to live behind those windows and
doors.

people who live behind the fancy front doors wonder
what it would be like to have uncomplicated
lives . . . fewer worries . . . productive children . . .
laughter in the home.

there are pluses and minuses everywhere.

when i was a child, it was a favorite form of
entertainment to take drives through the most
beautiful neighborhoods and just look at houses.

my daddy was a preacher. we always got the worn old
parsonages with chipped paint and bizarre colors
in the bathrooms.

especially at Christmas, i would stare at the mansions,
digging my chin into my arm on the rolled-down
window of the car, and wonder how satisfying it
must be to have one of those immense Christmas

trees, so ornately decorated, showing through
huge, wide-paned front windows . . . with probably
hundreds of wonderful presents.
my world seemed small . . . insignificant.

when jan and i were about twelve, my mother made
us matching dresses, with a border around the
skirt which said, "all that glitters is not
gold."
i would finger those words while sitting behind a
school desk. i really wanted, most earnestly,
to believe that . . .
but i was young and impressionable . . . and daddy
was a preacher in a rather small church . . . in a
foreign culture . . . and that made it difficult.
could those words really be valid?

one day in boston i ran across the street to see patti
zigelbaum and her miraculous new wonder of a
baby son. patti was such a beautiful, flawless,
captivating woman . . . living in an elegant
condominium.
she was married, and now had given birth to a healthy
child. she had everything!
i had tried to serve Jesus . . . to be true . . . to love.
it was my thirty-fourth year. where would i ever find
the right man? how could i ever have a child?

positives and negatives in everyone's life . . . good and
bad . . . easy and difficult . . . joy and sorrow . . .
laughter and tears . . . security and insecurity . . .
good days and rough ones.
usually only the surface shows. superficiality. the
front, dressed up and covered over to hide all
the lies underneath.

the suave, charming man who knows just what to say,
    and how.
the alluring woman who seems to have it all.
they may have lain, sleepless, in their beds for many
    hours the night before...lonely...empty.
the lovely, impeccably-dressed blonde...the envy of
    all the other women at the tea...may have
    come from a home where there was no love or
    warmth or sense of unity between her and her
    husband, or her children.

recently people have said to me:
    "ann, you do have *everything*. you travel the
    world...write books...run marathons. and now
    you have a good-looking, successful husband."
i *have* traveled extensively, written books, run seven
    marathons. i do have a man only God could have
    created so perfectly for me.
but my life is difficult at times. with recognition
    and praise come all the more criticism and
    judgment.
the demands and expectations are so much greater.
even, perhaps, the sorrows.
many people Jesus has called to be experiential
    authors are those He believes He can trust with
    more than the average amount of heartache and
    human suffering.
otherwise, what is there to write about that will touch
    people...with reality, heart, genuine compassion?
being vulnerable, transparent, and open are things i
    consider important. but there is a piece of mystery
    that i hold onto. a closet of broken pieces where
    the door is kept shut. it is mine alone...many
    tears, much failure, disappointments...injustices.
forgiven sins, but still wrongs that cannot be made

right or undone. they have taken their toll.

if my life were as ideal. . . as cut-and-dried. . . as it
   was perceived by that young woman who wrote to
   me, i would speak and write with indifference. . .
   with cold, remote heart. my life would be hollow,
   smug, superficial. . . and in time it would show.

it would kill the vision. . . the dream. . . the spirit.

i was asked by a Christian school in boise, idaho, to
   come as the "celebrity" to run in a jog-athon to
   raise money. i consented.

they were to send a private plane to pick up my
   husband and me in the afternoon, deliver us for
   an hour's run that evening, and bring us back
   home.

will had been working hard at the ranch, and i had
   been doing church calling all day.

by the time we boarded the small, single-engine
   plane, we were exhausted.

will casually mentioned that he had his running
   clothes with him.

"honey, you didn't bring those awful old khaki shorts,
   did you?"

"yes, they are all i have. . . besides, i like them."

"will, i hate them. they are so ugly."

it was not a nice thing to say. he really tried to
   please me.

but i wanted everyone who would be staring at us,
   watching to see whom ann kiemel had married,
   to like him.

everything went downhill from there.

a huge crowd had gathered at the park, around the
   mile-long, marked path. hundreds had come to
   see me run, and to run too. it was rather warm.
i am embarrassed to admit that i had eaten only some
   remnants of chocolate chip cookies i had baked
   for a neighbor man . . . and some caramel corn a
   lady had handed me while i was calling.
it was now six p.m. and i was to run for an hour . . .
   feeling empty and nauseated.

we arrived home at eleven p.m., after shaking hands
   and smiling, and being on display, and running
   eight miles — all within an hour. i was spent
   and terribly discouraged.
will had not looked the way i had wanted him to look.
   he was very quiet and remote (though he did run
   seven miles.)
i really was not myself. just two days before, i had
   returned from a ten-day speaking tour that had
   been scheduled long before i even knew will
   anderson.
too much time apart . . . not enough room for just the
   two of us.

and so that night i ended up saying things i deeply
   regret. things i did not mean . . . just harsh words
   out of a totally imperfect, exhausted earthen
   vessel.
"will, i hate you. i do not care about you.
   i don't even know why i married you . . . ."
   words like those.
sitting in the bathtub after midnight, shampooed
   head wrapped in a towel, i began to cry
   uncontrollably.
will walked in, picked me up out of the water,

dripping everywhere, and held me.
"woman, it is all right."
"oh, honey, it isn't. i am a bad person. i am no good.
    i didn't mean those words. Jesus must be sad.
and all those people at the run...honey, they believe
    in me. there were so many of them, and i didn't
    get a chance to express my love to all of them.
    i wanted to. i felt it, but...i can never be enough.
    not for you. not for Jesus. not for the world."

we stood there in the middle of the bathroom...one
    a.m. my heart was broken by my own badness, my
    inadequacy.
as i sobbed, will started praying.
"Father, God...i claim ann. this is my woman.
    i know she did not mean what she said.
i take responsibility for it. help her to understand
    that only YOU are enough for the world."

all through the night, i lay as close to will as
    i could get without pushing him out onto the floor.
    i patted him, held his arm, kissed his shoulder...
    and continued to cry off and on all night
    while he slept.
they were tears of sorrow...tears of gratitude for
    grace that is greater than my sin...that is a
    reality.
God's love...deeper than any black hole of failure.
and they were tears of thanksgiving for a husband
    who is a ROCK.

a new friend of mine, jay — now in a wheelchair
    for fifteen years — says there is no pain like
    the stab of regret.
of looking back and wishing one could have lived out

a vast number of moments differently . . . better.
of never, now, being able to change those times.

if we spend our lives being tempted by illusions, and
   confused, we will eventually have a life filled
   with great regret.
we will miss all the blessed moments, the celebrations,
   the carnivals. we will have failed to learn when
   to be happy . . . how to love ourselves and our own
   unique places in life.
we will get involved in relationships that are not God's
   idea . . . that will in time be destructive.
we will fail to give God time to thread a bright ribbon
   through a seemingly commonplace, ordinary life.

to cling to an illusion is to take a persistent walk
   toward death . . .
we must give God time to make the song live . . .
   and the miracle.

from jan to ann
   september 18, 1981
   dear ann . . .
initially, when i heard you were getting married,
   i was thrilled. what could be better than
   your actually having someone too . . . to love
   you, protect you, care for you?
we could share great times and go on vacations together.

then one night, perhaps three weeks later, it hit me.
i was being replaced. never had i had to share this
   special, intimate place in your life.
no one, ever, had come close to being more special to you
   than i. as little girls we had slept together

every night. poured out our hearts. confessed
our worst feelings to each other.
i had always held a predominant place in your life.

you really never got very close to others. i usually
had a close circle of friends, spent more time
being social.
you always had friends, but i was the only one you had
ever really turned to.
now i was losing this great place of significance.
you might be famous and have achieved things i never had,
but i was the one person you most loved.

that moment of awareness diminished me to sobbing
uncontrollably. i became overwhelmed with fear.
who would i be without this identity with you?
would i have any value without this special place?
now will would go with you. . . help you. . . support you.
he would share your dreams, and even to the world he
would become the person people would identify with you.

you had achieved great recognition in the world the
last few years, but i had married a strong, great
man. had borne two wonderful sons.
i did have something to offer you and myself that you
did not have, but now you would have that, too,
and because you have always done everything better,
you would be a better wife and mother.
i would have to be inferior on every level.

i would run. . . and pray for strength and God's help.
i wanted you to be happy. to have the best. i did not
want to feel these horrible, insecure feelings. . .
to darken your great happiness and excitement in
any way.

one morning, as i ran and wept, the Lord brought the words
    of this song:
    i will not forget thee or leave thee . . . in my
    arms i'll hold thee. in my arms, i'll fold thee.
    i am thy Redeemer. i will pilot thee.
the Lord brought great joy to me the week of the wedding.
i thoroughly experienced your joy . . . all the festivities.

in jackson hole, two weeks after your wedding, as we
    vacationed together in the tetons, i prayed for
    a third work of grace. nazarenes have two, but
    i needed more!
that third morning at breakfast the Holy Spirit orchestrated
    a conflict which led me into a profound time of
    transparency. for the first time in thirty-five years
    i began to share some of my feelings i had not ever
    articulated openly. i had to confess to this small
    group of friends my deep feelings of inferiority with
    you.
with others, i had been able to find a level of security.
    a feeling of value. but never in all my life had
    i been able to measure up to you.

at Christmas, no matter how hard i tried to do a great job
    of gift buying, you just had a knack for knowing what
    people needed. you bought in the best of taste.
i guess we ended up competing, but not because either one
    of us wanted to. i only wanted to be "as good as"
    you, not better.
when, on a few occasions, i felt equal to you, then you
    seemed sad. it was like only one of us could be
    good, and the other one felt forced to fall
    somewhere below.

i realized i must begin to come to terms with my own value

and identity. separate from you.
somehow, i had hung on to you for security. i must let go,
    and become whole all by myself.
you had always been my great leader. i actually needed you
    to be "better" because it challenged me to try harder.
    to achieve more, so people would not feel sorry for me.
i have accomplished more in life, ann, than i otherwise
    would have.
when i married tom, i continued to let you be my leader.
that day in jackson hole, the Holy Spirit began to reveal to
    me that not only did i need to come to terms with
    my own value, separate from you, but i also had to
    surrender my place in your life to will.
and i needed to turn totally to tom as my leader.
i felt i was hanging onto the side of a cliff, ready to
    drop and die somewhere below.
could i really trust tom and God to take care of me?
what if tom thought i should go one way, and you another?
would i have the courage to follow tom?

i remember saying to you, through great weeping,
"ann, i feel like you are in a ship, and i am on the shore,
    waving goodbye. we have had a great relationship
    for thirty-five years, and there will always be this
    great, deep, warm love and feeling, but you are
    going to sail away. we will never be the same again."

i chose, with enormous fear, but as a response of obedience,
    to let you go. there was a death in me.
it was like letting go of your hand, and letting you pass
    from life to death. i did not want to let loose,
    but i had to answer God's call.

ann, it may take me the rest of my life to truly respond
    and resolve these issues. in time, though, i know it will

be right and more beautiful than ever before.
i love you so much, ann.

jan

from ann to jan
    september 23, 1981
    oh, my dearest jan . . .
i am now a bride of four months.
today i received your letter.
    today i understood, more than ever
    in my life,
    why i value you so.

anyone who can be that real . . . that honest . . .
    so vulnerable . . .
merits the love and affection and devotion
    i have always had for you.

remember when we were little girls?
i always protected you, watched to make sure you
    did not fall down the steps.
    or miss out on your piece of the birthday cake.
for hours, at school, i would wait for the bells
    to ring for recess, so i could find you.
we knew kids would think it silly if we hugged,
    or held hands, or anything . . .
    but i could stand there in my saddle shoes
    and ponytail, and tell you my secrets.
    if i was scared of math class, or that some boy
    teased me . . . or i felt ugly.
    or that i spoiled the team's chance of
    winning the tag game.

jan, you are still the only one in the whole world

that i can tell anything to.
i am learning to bare my soul to will . . .
to trust him with my intimate, deep feelings.
but some things only you could possibly understand.
before there was conscious life, there was you . . .
with me. inside mom.
before breath or laughter or food or disappointment
or fear or growth or understanding or Jesus,
i knew you.
when we were children, i guess i was the leader.
but what is a leader without a follower?
not a leader.
no wonder i had such confidence and authority.
you believed anything i said.
you followed me with absolute trust.
you nurtured in me the assurance that Jesus and i,
together, could do anything.

remember, in it's incredible, *i wrote:*
someday, i hope we can write names in the sunset,
and ride bikes for hours, and rise early to care
for healthy babies.
someday i hope we have big fireplaces in old homes,
and families that create and laugh and share
and love
and dream.
God gave me you . . .
and you have made so much difference.
jan, my great person, i love you.
you have obeyed the inner calling to be whole.
to say "YES" to God's quiet voice.
and it makes you free.
you are my peer. my equal.
i will always wear a ribbon for you.

ann

from edith schaeffer to ann
september 26, 1981
dear ann...
what a relief you are! a piece of solid walnut with
no veneer.
i am always praying, "make me solid wood, Lord...
all the way through."
pure cotton, pure wool, pure linen, pure silk,
solid silver, the kind of brass that shines a
lifetime with tender polishing.

i love you for loving the children in boston and
for running so determinedly...
and i know all about being an alien and a minority!
i spoke chinese before english and loved sneaking out
at mealtime to the chinese homes in the compound
to eat forbidden food with chopsticks, as a
two- and three-year-old.

now...potatoes, and your intellectual husband and a prayer
for the child of the Lord's choice to be conceived
in the amazing moment when it will become a
person unique, different from whoever it might
have been a month before...or after! staggering!!
goodnight, with love,

edith

september 1981

my husband drives a green-and-white pickup.
    he tears across potato fields
    and over dirt roads.
i cough and hold my nose and wipe away streaks of

dust that settle over the seat and dashboard . . .
    and me.

"honey, can you bring the car and meet me in twin
    falls tonight? my truck broke down and i am
    leaving it here."

at nine p.m. this city girl crawls into a clean, polished
    car and starts across idaho's open country to
    meet the potato farmer, coming home from
    harvesting a special crop in oregon.
my hair is clean. i have packed a big lunch in a
    picnic basket.
i feel far away from every secure and familiar thing in
    my whole life.

"meet me at the 'ponderosa.' "

three hours later, at midnight, i see flashing neon
    lights next to the highway . . . fifty trucks . . . a
    lot of gasoline pumps.
walking into the coffee shop, i am startled by loud
    country music rolling out from the bar.
the restaurant is filled with authentic, tough-looking
    cowboys.
sitting at the counter — the only woman — i feel
    small and fragile. shy and utterly alone.
could those cowboys be as mean as they look?
    they stare at me. i bite my lip.
nothing on the menu looks good. the waitress is
    chomping gum and standing with an air of
    impatience.
"well . . . ya want some green tea? my gran'ma always
    gave that to me when i was sick . . . ."
her voice has a twang. she knows all about the fast-

living, hard-working, tough-surviving parts
   of the west. she has seen a lot . . . you can tell.
she is not afraid of anyone or anything.

i order tea and keep glancing around.
one cowboy — he must weigh 300 pounds — sipping
   coffee, his hat still on, is staring at me.
i turn around and look at the pies in the cooler and
   wish my husband would come.

''God, i like these people. they are different, but
   they are real. no veneer. no dolled-up,
   lace-trimmed, painted-over facade to impress
   anyone.
but Jesus, i feel so alone . . . so different. like when
   i was in hawaii. only now i am not overwhelmed.
   i have followed You a long way. i trust You.
   i am Yours. and now will's. i open my whole
   life to You.
will walks in the door . . . almost one a.m.
a fresh haircut makes him look ready to join the
   marines tomorrow morning. little streaks of
   scalp showing.
   funny, sort of . . . and awful.
''well, honey, i walked into this little barber shop
   and told the guy to give me a nice haircut for you.
i decided to read my book. when i put the book down,
   it was too late. all my hair was gone. he gives
   the same haircut to everybody.''

i am a bride of three months. have not seen my
   husband for seven days. no hair, but the same
   piercing black eyes, strong arms, even spirit.
to him, short hair or long hair — what did it matter?
he picks me up off the stool, hugs me, and carries me

out to the car. he proceeds to unload huge rolls
of drip irrigation tape and a pitchfork and
dirty overalls and tool box into my clean car.
standing in the dark parking lot, wind blowing my
hair and making me shiver — neon lights
making our skin a strange color — i put my
hands to my head.
"oh, no, i married a FARMER! honey, do you have
to take all that stuff home?"

will turns around and roars with laughter.
setting down the box of potatoes, he grabs me, pulls
me off the ground, and with only stars watching,
kisses me.
"woman, i missed you."
looking deep into my eyes, he starts to quote:
you fill up my senses. . . like a night in the forest. . .
like a walk in the rain. like a storm in the desert.
like a sleepy blue ocean. you fill up my senses.
come fill me again.
and i forget the loaded-down car with things only
a farmer would love.
or that it is late and i am exhausted.
or that this city girl was feeling alone in the wild west.

i only know this is my man.
God's perfect choice for me.
planned before life was in my lungs.
pondered in the heart of God when will was six
and i was three.
the program-in-the-making-for-years.

"God, i love this man!"

with my new little friend, angela, and a hereford calf.

we drive and talk and eat popcorn and homemade
    cookies and fruit and chicken sandwiches and
    cheese.
the potatoes had the nicest skins of any he had ever
    grown. were the biggest, finest variety.
there were not as many as he had hoped for.
    the prices were down. the investors might not
    get all their money back.
but it was God's program.

and i am his woman.
he trusts me with his heart.
no city slicker in the world could take his place
    in my life.

october 1981 — harvest

for will's potato harvest,
i rode on a combine. for hours and hours.
pulling out weeds and sticks.
picking up big clods of dirt and
    throwing them over. and rocks.
getting off the combine and learning what it
    means to work on your hands and knees
    in the dirt and dust.

i was the boss's wife. alone out there.
it was one time i did not sing to anyone.
i kept my mouth shut. smiled a lot.
worked *hard*. kept shaking the dirt and dust
    out of my hair and eyes.
and prayed
    for strength.

in my idaho office. . .backed up by mementos of races. the
picture is of my friend patti catalano.

for more wisdom in being will's woman.
for creative ways to bless the hired help.
(what could i bake them that they'd like?)
everyone was watching.
could the city girl make it?

by 8 p.m. i was frozen.
fingers and toes totally numb.
nose running. back tired.
stomach nauseated by the jerking machine
    and the moving belt of potatoes.
opposite motions.

i stumbled into my mother-in-law's kitchen,
    crying in pain. exhausted.
    hungry. incredibly cold.
she pulled off my muddy hiking boots.
had the sauna and whirlpool hot.
a wonderful dinner that made up for my misery.

i felt more love than ever for this man of mine . . .
    man of the earth . . . of sky and rain and
    outdoor air and sun.
strong hands. strong back. eternal optimism.
i understood better what it means to farm potatoes.
    to work the soil. to plant.
    to feed and water and nurse the roots.
    to pray for good weather . . . a good market . . .
    big yields.
then to pray for grace and wisdom when adversity
    strikes.
    to laugh hard. to work hard.
    to share freely.
    to be purely healthy and whole.

the dream still lives
back in boston . . . down a dark, forbidding street,
    next to a narrow, noisy, squeezed-in lane . . .
    in the basement of an old-but-sturdy building,
    there stands a little gymnasium to the honor
    and glory of Jesus Christ.
children play there . . . hockey, basketball, volleyball.
exercise classes for young mothers. Bible studies.
it was God's dream. He planted it in me. He made it
    live.

every week, i would save everything i could . . .
    sacrifice. old grandfathers would slip me
    dollar bills. young mothers would hand me
    fifty-cent pieces left over from grocery money.
    children started putting pennies in piggy banks.
i didn't ask for a dime from anyone, but money came
    in to match what i had.
once, in florida, i had been sharing my dream about
    the gymnasium with a crowd of 40,000 people.
after the meeting, i walked out to the waiting car and
    left.
the next morning i discovered that the crowds had
    found some trash cans, passed them around the
    auditorium and dropped money in . . . they sent
    me $12,000.
for days, i cried . . . overwhelmed.

each week the contractor and builder would come to
    my office to see how much money i had saved, and
    then they would decide what could be built the
    next six days.
i would sing them my little songs . . . tell them about
    Jesus . . . pray with them.
in the year and a half it took to get the money together .

and build this shining dream, they learned to
know much about Jesus. we laughed and cried
together many times.

steve and debbie forster, and four-year-old joshua,
are the directors at the gymnasium. they moved
right into the old building.
one night debbie called from boston, crying.
"ann, there is a rat, bigger than a cat, in our
apartment.
we can't catch it. ann . . . i'm scared!"
steve set traps . . . put poison around. they moved out
for a week, waiting.
one day, steve carved a spear out of wood. he was
going to destroy this culprit that was
disrupting their ministry to people in that
neighborhood.
for four hours, he sat on the kitchen counter, not
moving.
though the rat never showed up after the first couple
of visits, the poison disappeared.
they decided the rat had slipped away and died
somewhere.
though fearful, debbie brought little joshua, and they
moved back into their apartment.

every week, in boston, i would meet with the little girls
involved in the gym program . . . ten to
twelve-year-olds.
i'd buy them ice cream. read to them from the Bible.
sing them little songs. hold them on my lap. kiss their
faces. listen to them. take walks to fun places.
remind them that Jesus is love.

one sweet, fragile little girl . . . i won't share her

name . . . often looked hungry. so frail.
there was often no food in her house and she would not
    have eaten for awhile. i would send meat and
    fresh vegetables home to her worried mother.
once, secretly, i gave her money and sent debbie with
    her to buy something she needed to wear. two
    weeks later as i sat eating pizza with all the
    little girls, she ran around the table to me
    and kissed me.
her eyes were shining . . . she said nothing. she only
    radiated this great aura of joy that made the air
    sing. we were all caught up in it.
as i was hugging each girl good-night, i finally came to
    this girl. she had been waiting to be last.
she threw her arms around me, whispering with
    breathless excitement, "ann, oh, ann . . . i
    believe in MIRACLES.
    you like my jacket? you like my jeans?
    i bought them with your money. all my life, ann,
    other kids have teased me, until now. oh, ann,
    i love you."

squeezing this thin, wispy girl, i looked into her face
    and started singing . . .
    "freely, freely, you have received . . .
    freely, freely give.
    go in My name, and because you believe,
    others will know that i live. . . .
    you are only eleven, but you and Jesus can change
    the world."

people say, "ann, you don't *really* believe that, do
    you?"

yes, i do. i believe with all there is in me that one

small, genuine heart...plus a great God...
plus love...can change the world.
i am committed to that conviction...that hope.
whatever.

as i have mentioned, when will and i were married, a
choir of children from the gym program, dressed in
pastel robes and carrying bright fresh flowers,
preceded me down the aisle.
they filled old park street church with their
childish voices..."God loves you...and we
love you...and that's the way it should be...."
when i joined will at the front of the church, they sang,
whither thou goest, i will go...
where thou lodgest, i will lodge...
i watched each face. i saw the love in those piercing
dark eyes. those children are a part of me...of the
air i breathe...the burden i carry.
they are the sunrise for all tomorrow's horizons.
i am committed to them for life, whatever it costs,
wherever it leads me.

now i live in idaho. those children are still growing up
in the tough inner city of boston.
they are there to take my place...to carry the dream.
to remind that corner of the world that Jesus is
love.
now that i am gone, they are the voices, crying out in
the asphalt jungle that Jesus changes
EVERYTHING.

steve and debbie and joshua are still there...at nine
salutation street, north boston. i use my speaking
money to support them.
i try to stop in to see them every month...to be there

for the children, too.
clothes hang on old lines across the streets.
sunshine is stolen and hidden by worn old buildings.
cars screech and honk. dogs bark.
but over the roofs and across the sky is the sound of
    children's laughter . . . of music . . . and games.
and there is beauty . . . a rainbow . . . a hallelujah
chorus.

autumn 1981

my husband is, of all people i have ever known, the
    most avid reader . . . a persistent questioner.
by the time he married me, he had read all the books
    he could on marriage and sexual intimacy and
    the family. he had flown to different parts of
    the country, spending days talking to people who,
    he had heard, have outstanding marriages.
his was going to be the perfect . . . the most unique
    marriage in history . . . and his wife the most
    satisfied woman in the world.
thirty-eight-year-old potato farmer and thirty-five-
    year-old professional woman marry, enter a
    fairy-tale existence, and live happily ever after.

well, in this situation, too, it seems we have to give
    God time to blend our lives.
one of the first things i did in our new home was to
    open the door of will's closet . . . and find his
    wardrobe.
it contained the most terrible array of
    fifteen-to-twenty-year-old clothes i had
    ever seen.
"honey, we *must* get rid of these clothes. all of them."

"what do you mean? i love my clothes. they have been
   my friends."
will's mother, sisters, and friends tell me that they
   have tried for years to inspire him to buy new
   things. they did their shopping in new york
   or dallas.
will's philosophy, however, was: the clothes were good
   fifteen years ago . . . they are not worn out . . . so
   they are good today.
he has finally given me the honor of choosing one
   garment each week, to pull out and "lose." it
   may take a long time, but it is something to
   work toward.

recently i had a speaking engagement in los angeles.
will was able to accompany me on this particular trip,
   so on the way home we stopped in san francisco
   to visit my parents.
on sunday morning, my father — seventy-four, and
   retired from the ministry — was filling in for
   a pastor on vacation.
   it was a small, enthusiastic church.
will and i were going to go with them. we had been
   asked to give our testimonies before flying
   home in the afternoon.
my husband's shoes were as bad as his clothes. his best
   ones, an expensive pair of wing tips — only fifteen
   years old — were badly creased.
shortly before we were married, i had bought him
   loafers — just good, leather, ivy-league penny
   loafers. i have always felt shoes said a *lot*
   about a person.
as we were getting ready to leave the guest bedroom to

go to church — my parents in the car, waiting — i
looked down to see that will was wearing one of his
pairs of old black shoes. i was horrified.
"honey, you aren't going to wear those old shoes, are
you?
oh, honey, please wear your loafers. they make you
look like you know where you are going. like you
are thirty-eight instead of seventy-five!"

will roared with laughter. "ann, these shoes have
traveled many miles with me. i like them. they
feel good and i am going to wear them today . . . ."

i frowned. it was just inconceivable to me.
"honey, please . . . ." my voice whined out the plea.

he hesitated.
"i will make a deal with you. if you quit drinking all
diet pop, so we can have healthy kids, you can
have these shoes right now."
diet drinks were my favorite way to save calories. no
way did i want to waste calories on what i drank.
i wanted to save them for cake and cookies and
ice cream and rolls.
however, it did not take me one second to decide. my
husband represented me to the world, and the shoes
made the wrong kind of statement.
"honey, i promise. no more diet drinks. now give me
those shoes . . . ."

he sat down on the edge of the bed, untied his shoes
and held them a couple of minutes.
"you've gone a long way with me!"
and with a sentimental look he handed them over
and slipped into the loafers, smiling broadly.

"mother," i said as we got into the car. "i left will's
old black shoes in the bedroom. take them to the
salvation army . . . or burn them . . . or anything!"

about a week later, my mother called to say she had
started to throw them out, but just could not.
she had put them in a bag and was going to leave
them at a nearby thrift shop, but it came to
her that these were like old friends to will.
"will, your shoes are in the closet here. anytime you
come to see us, you can wear them."

after a two-week honeymoon, we settled into our
brand-new little sun valley chalet home.
the second evening, i suggested that i needed to go
grocery shopping, and will said he would go
along.
i was thrilled. it is always fun just to be with him . . .
for us to do things together.
pulling out a grocery cart, i started moving down the
aisles, piling in all kinds of things for our
little kitchen. we needed everything.
as i would put an item into the basket, will would
pick it up and, still walking, start reading
the ingredients listed on the label.
"honey, this has sodium in it . . . and artificial food
coloring."
or "ann, we must not get this product here. the
health food store will have the freshly-ground,
whole wheat variety."

now let me say that i do undertand why will is so
aware of diet.

his healthy, robust father suddenly came down with
   stomach cancer, and after a slow, painful illness,
   died about five years ago. although the rest of
   the family is apparently in perfect health, they
   have all become very conscious of the fact that
   most americans eat for pleasure, not for health.
however, i felt insecure and worried about my
   cooking.
though my mother is a tremendous cook . . . and i
   think a girl tends to be like her mother . . . i had
   lived alone for so long and had been on the
   road so much, that i didn't have much
   confidence in my own cooking — apart
   from homemade cookies and popcorn!
above all, i wanted to be a fantastic cook for this big
   healthy, robust man i was so crazy about.

after about five aisles of having will pull out half of
   the things i had placed in the basket and replace
   them on the shelves, i was destroyed.
he made me feel that i was about to poison him.
he could tell, i guess, by the look on my face that i was
   getting desperate. he wrapped his arm around me,
   hugged me and winked.
i looked up and said quietly,
   "go home, will anderson. i mean it . . . GO
   HOME."

we decided it was best that we not shop for groceries
   together.
i have learned much from him about good eating
   habits . . . and he has come to trust my cooking.
it has become one of the most fulfilling parts of my
   marriage . . . creating healthful, exciting meals for
   my husband, here in this small country town

where everyone eats homemade bread and
home-grown vegetables.

will's hair is very coarse and naturally curly.
    i like his hair short . . . but not
    extremely so.
my husband totally accepts people as they are,
    and has never built a person's value
    around his or her personal appearance . . .
so it has never really registered with him that
    how his hair is cut is important.

one time, while visiting him in idaho falls before
    the wedding, i said,
    "will, let's go to the barber shop together.
    i would like to meet your barber."
    "sure!" he seemed enthusiastic.
    what could he lose?

the barber told me that for years, will would come in
    from the ranch . . . good book in hand . . .
    sit in the chair, and ask for a haircut.
    no specifics. no directions.
    he would not even look at it when the haircut
    was done.
    he would thank the barber, give him a large tip,
    and walk out until it seemed he should go again.

all you married women . . . i wonder if you understand
    how i feel when, the last three times my husband
    has walked out of a barber shop, he was nearly
    scalped. i mean . . . he has not even looked like
    my husband.
he is so much more secure than i am, and his values

are all in the right areas.
he has promised me not to read a book the next time,
    but to try to watch the barber.
    smile. sigh.
    prayers. quiet hope.

we had been married for about four months, and one
    day i said, "will, let's invite the langlies for
    dinner. they have done so much to help us get
    settled. there would be six of us. what do
    you think?"
"great idea! do it! let's have them come early, about
    six p.m., because i leave early tomorrow morning
    to harvest the crop in oregon."
all day i cooked. cream cheese with shrimp hors
    d'oeuvres. fresh baked chicken. jezebel sauce.
    rice and green chile casserole. homemade yeast
    biscuits and cinnamon rolls. salad. giant
    chocolate chip cookies and brownies.
the house was spotless. the table set. fresh flowers.
the guests arrived at six p.m. — on time — but no
    will anderson.

i smiled . . . offered cold drinks . . . tried to keep the
    food warm, while wondering, with anger building
    up behind my cool, casual front, where my
    husband was . . . he who had suggested six p.m.
    to start with.
at six-forty he walked in. trouble with the pickup, he
    said. brought a man with him to work on it. could
    he have dinner too?

my grandma's famous chocolate chip cookie recipe . . .
in my kitchen. i love to cook.

earlier, i had suggested that we make ice cream in the
   six-quart electric freezer we had received for
   a wedding gift. though we had never tried it, i
   thought it would be fun, and had made the cookies
   especially to go with ice cream.
however, i was thinking of its having been made ahead
   of time, and in the freezer when they arrived.
will was to pick up the ice and salt on the way home.
considering his late arrival, i had shelved that idea,
   but when he walked in, his arms were loaded with
   three huge bags of ice and salt crystals.
before we had even said grace at the table, he had
   dragged the freezer out, with the direction book.
meanwhile, everyone waited, nearly starved.
finally he laid the book down, had us join hands and
   say grace about fifteen minutes into the meal, he
   disappeared into the garage to help bob, returning
   with black grease all over his hands, shirt, and face.

as soon as dinner was over, he called gordie, our
   guest, over.
   "let's make this ice cream ourselves."
it was obvious to me that nothing was going to deter
   will from this project.
if i had been a more experienced hostess, i probably
   would have handled it with much more relaxed
   grace, but i was very insecure about being the
   "perfect" wife and homemaker. i so wanted it
   to be a wonderful evening.
i pulled out whipping cream and half-and-half and
   eggs and fresh raspberries. . . i hurriedly loaded
   the dishwasher and cleaned off counters while
   these two men got a recipe book and started
   to work.
occasionally gordie would be left with some

128

instructions from will, and will would dash
    off to the garage. . .and bob. . .and the pickup.
an hour later the ice cream was still soft, and we
    dished up bowls of the most unusual tasting soft
    ice cream.
later, as we told our sweet guests good-night, will put
    his greasy, black hand in mine.
"honey, they are great people, aren't they? what a
    quality evening!"

i was so angry i could not speak. quality evening?
    i was utterly exhausted and in shock.
"will anderson, i have never seen you be such a
    terrible host. i am NEVER going to entertain
    again."
i cried. i pulled on running shoes and shorts and ran
    through the quiet residential streets, screaming,
    "Jesus, sometimes marriage isn't so easy."

when i came in, will was lying across the bed on his
    back. . .very sober.
"ann, my business can go down the tubes. . .and
    everything else. but what you think of me matters.
    i cannot believe Jesus thinks this situation is
    quite this serious."

will really loves people. he just happens to
    be more thing-and-goal oriented.
he had wanted our guests to have a meaningful
    evening just as much as i did.
we both fell asleep, exhausted.
the world looked much more sane the next morning.

will has won my whole heart. he is his own man.
    he is wild and reckless and brilliant and refined

all in one male body.
he is the greatest adventure of my entire life.
but he is a different human being from me. as
    independent and strong-willed as i am.

i want to report that life is life.
nothing, really, is a fairy-tale.
life gets better and better, and harder and harder.
    i read that somewhere . . . and it is so true.
i read a letter to abby van buren . . .
"dear abby: i am forty-four and would like to meet a
    man my age without any bad habits. rose."
"dear rose: so would i."

i have been single. now i am married.
i have lived on both sides of the fence, and would not
    trade either one. for thirty-five years, Jesus
    allowed me to be creative and fulfilled in a
    unique, public way. now He has blessed me with
    so much excitement and challenge under one roof.
i have a man with flawless character and a worldwide
    vision to feed the poor in china and africa.
he holds me in his arms and sings me old fraternity
    songs and loves ice cream as much as i do.
he is a great thinker and a stimulating
    conversationalist, and can do *anything*
    out-of-doors well.

but there are dirty clothes in the closet,
    and toothpaste in the sink . . .
    and rolls of drip-irrigation tape in the garage.
i want everything neat and in perfect order.
he is far more casual and relaxed.

only one thing is the real secret to a happy, centered,

fulfilled life: making Jesus LORD.
if He is our greatest desire...
if we delight in HIM...
then we can be positive and radiant and joyful and
    whole wherever He chooses for us to serve.
on the bottom line of life, it is
    Jesus and you and i...and love.
being happy and contented in HIS plan.

november 1981

everywhere people ask me, "how do you like living
    out west?"
well, it's a new place.
no longer do i live in an apartment building in
    downtown boston, but in a normal, regular
    neighborhood.
one does not pass others going to the elevator...
    or in the lobby of the building.
nice houses...quiet streets...professional.
(though will's work is at the ranch, the home place,
    and in oregon, we live right in town. we bought
    a charming, snug new home.)

for a long time i could not see any runners around
    idaho falls. day after day i would run, in the
    heat, alone.
for several weeks we did not have a car...only will's
    pickup which he took out every day.
i would run to the offices downtown...to the grocery
    store...to see my mother-in-law...to pick up the
    dry cleaning.
it was not quite as picturesque and charming as
    running along the charles river.

will encouraging me to learn to drive a tractor.

also, when i lived in boston, though i knew almost
    everyone in my waterfront neighborhood, they did
    not see me as any kind of celebrity.
after several years, the word did get around that i
    wrote books and traveled. some would see me on
    television or find one of my books in some
    restaurant book rack.
but there were few evangelical Christians around,
    so my identity was very vague to people.
i was just "ann." period. a person.
i worked at keeping a low profile.
i sang little songs and tried to love others in creative
    ways, but i did not talk about my public life.

moving to idaho falls changed everything.
suddenly i was a celebrity of sorts right in my own
    neighborhood.
Christians, compacted into a small radius — not
    used to having an author move in — were
    suddenly very enthusiastic about my coming.
everyone was so warm. so kind. knocking on my door
    to meet me. . .to leave a note.
stopping me in the grocery store or bank to tell me
    they really appreciated my books.
i was always deeply grateful and happy about their
    kind response.

but suddenly, here i was, feeling again that i could
    never measure up. never be perfect enough for
    everyone.
that everywhere people were watching.
that they had enormous expectations of what "ann
    kiemel" was going to do with this city that needed
    God.
people would say, "oh, ann, have you found lots of

children in this city to love?'' . . . ''are you able
to share Jesus with all those we have never been
able to?''
this overwhelmed me. never had i claimed to be an
angel or a miracle worker.
i have always awakened with that same, simple
prayer, ''Jesus, i am just ann, but i am *one*.
please make me creative in this corner today.''
and all my life Jesus has opened the doors.
directed my steps.
my sharing has always been spontaneous. from my
heart.

more and more i began to find myself smiling on the
outside, but becoming very guarded.
i would fly every week to speaking engagements
(dates that were already booked before i knew i
would be married), and was the center of
attention.
then i would fly home to find myself in the same
fishbowl.
on top of that, i was wanting so much to be a perfect
wife for will anderson.
say all the right things. cook everything he loved.
keep a perfect house. smile sweetly.
be totally submissive.
''to submit'' was a part of my marriage vow, and i had
put that in because i really believed that to be
God's will for our home.
it was a lot easier to say it at the marriage altar than
to live it out, day after day, in my marriage.

will came in one saturday and said, ''honey, could you
pack a quick lunch? let's go canoeing.''
''canoeing? honey, i have never been canoeing. i'm so

horseback riding with my little friend angela.

tired. what do i have to do in the canoe?"

"help paddle, you silly goose."

i just wanted to lie in bed or read a good book.
or sit across from will and talk about something deep.
who wanted to drive several hours to *canoe?*
submission.
yes, Lord. as unto You.
i packed a lunch. pulled on old shorts
    and a sweatshirt, and we headed out.

we were canoeing downstream (and honestly, i was
    loving it.
    it was just getting there and starting it that
    was hard for me).
suddenly i noticed a huge moose running through
    the grass along the bank.
this piece of the snake river was far away from
    everything. remote.
will would point out a bald eagle up on a high branch,
    or some other rare bird.

casually, i said, "honey, a moose can't hurt you, can
    it?"

"sure, it can attack . . . but you just have to be
    careful."

no sooner had will said that, but our canoe rounded a
    little bend, and standing there in the water,
    inches from us, was the biggest moose will said
    he had ever seen — with her two babies. i was
    terrified.

"ann," will said in a very quiet, level voice. "put your
   paddle on the other side of the canoe."

"no . . . i won't . . . honey, turn this canoe around.
   right now. please. . . ." my voice was shaking.
   i thought life was finished for me.

"ann, do as i told you . . . shift the paddle to the other
   side."
though i could tell he was surprised and extremely
   cautious, he was steady and commanding.

"please don't make me move, will." i was crying by
   this time. "the paddle will shake the boat if i try
   to change it. i'm afraid she's going to get me. you
   should just be happy you are in the back of this
   canoe."

but very slowly, trying to trust this man who was now
   my husband, i carefully lifted the paddle over to
   the other side. we hardly breathed . . . waiting.
after some time, the mother moose and her twin
   babies turned and stepped out of the water
   and ran silently through the tall grass.
   relief. air to breathe. a fast smile and a kiss
   blown to will.
   "Jesus, thanks!"

because we hope to have children very soon, will has
   felt i should cut down on my running — to only
   four to six miles a day.
however, for someone who is used to doing ten to
   fifteen miles a day, faithfully, it was very difficult.

i had never thought it was worth even getting dressed
    to run if i was going to run only three or four
    miles.

again . . . submission. trusting my husband.
    listening to him. letting him be God's voice to me.
    following the chain of command.

submission to someone else is quite a challenge when
    one is used to being independent and traveling
    all over the world for years and years. a
    self-starter and a self-thinker.

some people don't agree about this philosophy . . . and
    that is okay . . . but for me, i know this is
    right.

there cannot be two presidents of the same
    corporation.
    just one . . . and a vice-president.

frankly, i do not view one position as better than the
    other.

only different. special job descriptions and roles for
    each.

bonhoeffer says, *no one should be surprised at the difficulty*
    of faith. if there is some part of one's life
    where he (she) is consciously resisting or disobeying
    the commandment of Jesus, go rather and be reconciled
    with your brother. renounce the sins which hold you
    fast . . . and then you will recover your faith.

one night, will came in and said, "honey, instead of
    taking all our neighbors to see *joni* at the seven p.m.
    showing, we are going at nine p.m. it just works out
    better for everyone that way."

nine p.m.?

that was so late. already that day, i had gotten up early,

138

run six miles. . .baked cookies for people. cleaned
house, done four loads of clothes, answered mail in
the office for hours, fixed a big dinner.
the thought of getting home after eleven p.m.—
when the next day looked just as demanding —
threw me.
as i stirred something on the stove, my heart was
racing, my face reddened. . .angry but saying
little.
suddenly the thought came to me, "submit.
relinquish."

i remembered reading in *celebration of discipline* by
richard foster:
every discipline has its corresponding freedom.
what freedom corresponds to submission? it is the
ability to lay down the terrible burden of always
needing to get your own way. the obsession to
demand that things go the way we want them to go.
in. . .discipline. . .we are released to drop the matter,
to forget it. frankly, most things in life are
not nearly so important as we think they are.

suddenly, praying as i stirred, i asked God to forgive
me for always wanting my own way. for always
thinking i knew what was best. i relinquished
the evening into His hands, and forgot it.
will and i had a leisurely, wonderful dinner. . .
unrushed, stimulating conversation. a good nap.
getting up around eight p.m. to get dressed to go, i
realized that i had gotten everything i wanted
anyway. . .and was refreshed and ready to take
people from our neighborhood to a film with
an exciting Christian message.
it was a super evening, and i felt terrific the next day.

never have i been what one might call a "crier"...
but since marrying and moving to idaho, there
have been a few nights when will has had to
hold me while i cried long into the night...
very frightened.
i have been missing...not boston, though i love that
great city immensely...but my children there...
dear, close friends, whom i had learned to
trust intensely.
crying because i felt so lost...so unlike "ann."
so unsure of my new place, my new mission.
so obviously human and inadequate, and failing
every day in little ways before my husband's
very eyes.

for awhile, i began to lose my grip on grace and faith.
all my life, i had been happy wherever i had lived...
in whatever new circumstances He placed me.
now i wanted instant transition, instant mission and
challenge...and certainly, instant perfection.
then, once more, i would be *good*...and thus, safe and
loved.
generally two things are said about a public person:
things too good to be true.
things too bad to be true.
i know this...Jesus does not choose the BEST people
for His service. there are thousands, i know,
more deserving than i of all the opportunities
He has brought my way.
i have come to believe He chooses the weak
instruments to ensure that His power
might be more fully manifested.
john the baptist said, *"as He grows greater, i must grow
less."*
i must be less and less occupied with self.

embroidered pillows...
gifts from people who love us.

it is now only my fifth month as a bride, in a new
   place, and i am beginning genuinely to feel the
   wonder of this fresh calling . . .
   but everything takes time.

each day, as i would be out running, i would pass the
   home of a man who sat in a wheelchair on his
   front porch.
i would run by and wave. one day, i ran up to him
   and said, "hi, i am ann. i'm new here.
   there's a little song i bet you would love . . ."
before he could answer, i had reached out and taken
   his hand, and started singing,
   God loves you . . . and i love you . . .
   and that's the way it should be . . . .
he proceeded to tell me that fifteen years ago he
   contracted multiple sclerosis. a year later his
   wife divorced him. now he cannot walk or
   feed himself.
once he was a construction superintendent . . . now
   completely confined to a wheelchair . . . one meal a
   day, at noon, when a nurse comes in to feed him.
i started baking him cookies every week.
then will and i would buy ice cream and will would
   feed him while we visited.
sometimes we put him in our car and take him
   somewhere. or feed him popcorn.
i always sing him a little song and tell him the plan of
   salvation . . . that Jesus will make him more free
   than the ability to walk. or a new body.
but i do not push. or force. just love him.

another morning, as i ran up to my front door, i
   turned and saw two ladies coming around the
   corner . . . running slowly. i raced out into the street.

"hi. . .i'm ann. do you run every day?"

"are you the lady who just moved in here? the
    marathoner?"

"yes. . . ."

"oh, we have heard about you. we are thrilled you are
    here. we are pretty slow, but we would love to
    have you run with us."

i went into my kitchen and fell on my knees in tears.
    thanksgiving. excitement. Jesus had helped
    me find some runners. . .and in my own
    neighborhood.
i have run with them every morning i am home. i do a
    few miles, slower, with them. . .and then pick up
    my pace and add a couple of miles alone.
one morning mildred said, "there is a lady a couple of
    streets over who is a walker. she and some others
    want us to come to breakfast thursday."
it was so lovely. cinnamon rolls and eggs and hot
    chocolate.
mormon, catholic, protestant, unchurched.
i shared who i was and how i felt and what i wrote
    about. . .and about my living Christ.

carol and mildred wanted to run a half-marathon
    (13.2 miles) that was being held here in idaho falls.
it was going to be on a weekend i would be away,
    speaking, but i began to work with them. . .
    gave them training hints. . .talked
    about diet.

will and his ranch man, glenn, working on a spray boom.
big sky . . . rich soil.

one saturday morning, i ran them through twelve
   miles . . . sang them my little songs . . . prayed
   with them when they got tired.
though i was not here to run with them, they both
   finished the race, and carol won first place in
   her division.
last week they had a coffee for me, inviting
   twenty-five women from our neighborhood
   to meet me. it was their own idea. i
   was delighted.
they asked me questions. i answered . . . and listened
   to them as they told me who they were.
i told them, "like many parts of the country, this area
   has people who believe many different things.
i want you to know that whoever you are, i am your
   friend.
i will laugh and cry with you. or read the Bible to your
   children and sing songs to them.
or eat cookies and talk over your dreams with you.
i must tell you that Jesus is the center of my life . . .
      my Song every day . . . but if you do not believe,
      i will still stand with you always . . . and be there."

tears and belonging and warm conversation.
laughter and sweet rolls and hot punch and new
   beginnings.
ladies i would never have met had i not married will,
   obeyed God, and followed Him to a new corner.

recently i became the church caller. you see, our
   church is very small — only about fifty — and
   we meet in a school. it is a community
   church — nondenominational,
   evangelical. will attended there before we married.
it occurred to me that although i am on the road on

some sundays, i could visit people during the week.
then they would feel more comfortable with me and
think of me as just a normal, everyday
person — not a speaker or writer.
pam, my secretary, goes with me and studies the map
so she can tell me where to drive.
we hold babies on our laps. deliver cookies. pray
quiet prayers. sometimes sing a little song.
it seems that every day i am running into new people
in my world who do not know Jesus, or go to
any church . . .
and once more, dreams dance all over the walls
of my heart.

love song
cool early morning.
crystal-clear lake.
the Son of Man, standing on the shore.
tired, wet, discouraged fishermen pulling in their
empty nets.

several days before, around three in the afternoon,
with pain and agony so intense and shocking
that heaven and earth and hell were shaken . . .
that same Son of Man became the Savior of the world.
the atonement for our sin. the Hope for our sorrow
and disappointment.
our eternal Song in the night.

"have you caught anything?"
"no, sir. hard night. no fish."
"try the other side."
while they did, He cooked their breakfast — fresh
fish on a hot fire. a rich aroma carried by the

new morning air.
He saved men's souls. He satisfied hungry stomachs.

"peter," with quiet, commanding voice.
"peter, do you love Me?"
reckless, strong, rugged peter...eyes dark with
    emotion.
"oh, Lord...it is You. Lord, of course i love You."
"peter...."
"yes, Lord...."
"do you *really* love Me?"
"Lord, why do you ask Me that again?
    my Lord, i love You."
"peter, people say they love Me. they talk about it.
    they preach it. they write it. they flaunt it.
    they say they do all kinds of things because
    they love Me...but peter, do you love Me?"
"Lord, i have meant to. i have wanted to. i have tried.
often i have worked hard and spent a lot of time
    sharing my love for You with others. i wish i
    had done more.
but Lord, i am so human and imperfect. i even denied
    knowing You. but i love You.
with all there is in me, i love You...."

Jesus stooped to turn the fish over. to breathe into the
    fire and quicken the coals.
clean morning sky and a silent breeze...and the smell
    of cold fish still flopping in the nets...a
    lot of them...from casting nets on the other side.
the sun climbing higher now, warming tired backs
    and sore limbs.

"peter, i am going to the Father.
    take care of My sheep. watch over them.

love them. forgive them easily.
  be patient with them. . . and merciful.
i am counting on you, peter.
as i love you, so you must love them.''

Lord, it is i. ann. . . the woman with the dream.
sometimes, Lord, i have loved You for all the
  wrong reasons.
and now that i am married, i realize all the more
  how inadequate my love has been.
  how self-centered. self-directed.
when i am supposed to be loving will, even as i love
  You, i fall so far short. want my own way.
  resist submission. rebel.
but Lord, count on me, too. . . along with all the
  other peters.
if my desire and fervent, earnest heart, can give You
  freedom to love through me,
  i am here, Lord.
  i am here.
and i love You, Lord.

''*delight thyself also in the LORD, and He shall give thee
  the desires of thine heart. . .* '' psalm 37:4.
Jesus became the desire of my heart. . .
  and suddenly, out of the mists of all
  the unknown tomorrows. . .
He brought will.
and a new, wide place to grow.

no easy answers
four weeks after coming to idaho, on a breezy
  saturday afternoon, i went bike-riding with my
  secretary, pam.

i borrowed a ten-speed from laurie, our bookkeeper.
will was at the home place, cultivating potatoes, so
   i suggested we bike out there and take him a big
   cold drink and then ride back into town.
"honey," i called across the rows of potatoes. "i have
   some cold juice for you."
in a few minutes he was down at our end of the row. i
   handed him a huge pitcher of ice cold punch and
   said, "honey, could pam and i ride the tractor with
   you? i have *never* been on one."

"sure. climb on up...."
we rode a few rows with him, coughing through huge
   swirls of dust flying everywhere. holding my legs
   just right so as not to get them caught in the
   machinery. then we hopped off. i hugged him and
   off we headed for home.

as we were riding low on our bikes, due to the strong
   winds, a speeding car came tearing around a
   corner. the driver was going so fast that
   instead of turning into his own lane, he
   swung out into the lane where i was riding.
i knew the car was going to hit me, but i couldn't do
   anything.
   i simply watched, helpless, as it hit me head on...
   my face taking the full impact.
my body was thrown into the air and back onto the
   pavement.
blood and teeth swam in my mouth and my face felt as
   if there was nothing there. i sat in the street,
   stunned, while a crowd gathered with blankets.

"please, someone...get my husband."

the bicycle, with the wheel twisted from the accident.
Jesus watches over me.

"who is he?" a man asked.

"will anderson."

"i know him. i'll do it and bring him to the hospital."

lying on the cold table in the emergency room of a
  hospital i had never seen before, i wondered what
  this meant.
it was such a terrifying experience. no one would even
  give me a mirror so i could see if i had a face.
they blotted my face with wet towels and assured me
  that the doctors and my husband would be there
  shortly.
pam waited anxiously in the hall.

before i had even arrived at the hospital, i had begun
  thanking God.
"Jesus, i do not know what this means, but i know
  You are love. i trust You. i know you are with
  me. i thank You even for this because i know
  You can work it out for my good."
my husband walked in within minutes, it seemed.
his doctor, whom we both love and have confidence
  in, had called a plastic surgeon . . . the only
  one in idaho falls. he had moved here only
  six months before.
a fine oral surgeon came also, because there were
  nerve endings hanging from my upper gum.
i had thirty-eight stitches in my face . . . my two front
  teeth knocked out. a lot of shots. a lot of pain.
  big, ugly bruises.
  but no broken bones.
an absolute miracle, the doctors say, that i lived,
  and without being a bunch of broken pieces.

every day i felt so much joy. never once did i complain
about the pain or the way i looked. i was so happy
to be alive. to be whole. to know i would heal
without any bad scars.
when i went to see the plastic surgeon two weeks later,
he said, ''ann, never in my experience as a
plastic surgeon have i seen your kind of
healing. you definitely have connections.
i could never take credit for this.''
within three weeks, one would never know i had even
been in an accident, nor that i had had all
those stitches.
there is a pink mark on my lip. the surgeon said he
could correct it, but for me, it is a scar to
remind me of this great thing Jesus did.
never before had i known He loved me *that* much.
it hurt a lot, but i got to share Jesus with the doctors
and with the boy who hit me . . . and with many
others.

i have never tried to say, ''i understand all of life.''
i do not.
there are dark, narrow, painful places.
crowded paths where some can hardly walk or even
stumble along . . . or breathe. where human hearts
find life so painful that desperate cries fill the
night hours.
''Jesus, where are You? are You there? do You hear
me? will i ever laugh again? can the tide ever
change? oh, Jesus . . . why are You so removed
from me?''
tears soak pillows. hearts sometimes turn hard and
cold and hollow. the dream dies. the hope

dissipates. the soul shrivels with doubt
and despair.

some of my favorite people are mike and jan
   sonnenberg. young. vivacious. enthusiastic.
mike is a professor at an eastern college. they are
   parents of three wonderful little children.
several years ago, they were en route to new
   hampshire for a vacation, traveling in
   different cars.
at a toll booth at the massachusetts/new hampshire
   border, a gasoline truck crashed into the back
   of mike's car, and flames burst out.
from the other car, jan and her
   daughter watched the accident . . . jan knowing her
   baby son was in the back seat in a baby holder.
through raging flames, mike pulled little joel out, but
   he was charred beyond recognition . . . so severely
   burned that there was little hope of survival.

many surgeries, prayers, and months later, this
   brave, determined, tough little boy was removed
   from the critical list . . . a valiant survivor.
i can't say i understand. i do not. never have i been
   through what joel has. but there is a stream of love
   that pours around and in me and moves across the
   miles to where joel is.
the sonnenbergs and i met because joel was at
   shriner's burn institute in boston. they
   were familiar with my books and called my
   office to see if we might have lunch
   together sometime.
i took chocolate chip cookies to joel.
sipped hot chocolate with jan in the crowded coffee
   shops near the hospital.

looked into mike's face and prayed. . .wondering how
   much sorrow one man could carry and still move
   through the daily routines.

joel, now past three years of age, has no hands. . .no
   nose, ears, or toes. he was burned over 98 percent
   of his body. his skin is severely scarred. . .he
   must wear a helmet to cover a hole in his skull.
for years joel will have to make trips to the boston
   burn center. there is always pain.
in one of his operations, joel's doctors did
   some surgery which would give him
   a thumb.
the day before the cast was to be removed,
   the family gathered around, excited.
   this might be the only finger he ever has
   in this life.
"joel, i hear something," exclaimed mike.
   "a little voice is coming from inside your cast!"
"my thumb!" joel replied. "it says, 'get me
   out of here quickly.' "
"tomorrow you will see your thumb, joel."
"fingers!" blurted joel.
"finger," his parents repeated.
"five fingers!" joel retorted.
"no, son. . .*one,"* mike explained.
"not five fingers?" cried joel in disbelief,
   as he looked at everyone's hands.
"daddy, mommy, and jami have five fingers," he
   argued.
"Joel, you are going to have a thumb, and it is
   going to be so neat. it will help you
   pick up things and do many other things."
"me want five fingers!" he cried over and over.
"joel, you will have five fingers in heaven.

someday you will have them.
but right now the doctor is giving you a thumb."
the cast came off.
there was a birthday party for joel's thumb.
with cake and a grand celebration.

other children don't understand his appearance. . .
one day as joel played in his front yard,
several children came up.
"you are disgusting!" "you are ugly!" "why does
that kid wear a monster mask?"
and they ran away, screaming.
joel's parents are often exhausted, emotionally and
physically. they weep for their child, so
hurt and abused and misunderstood by the world.
they long for strength and wisdom to teach him
courage. . . a brave, stout heart. . . faith. to keep
him from learning bitterness. to nurture trust —
beyond reason and understanding — in a loving
God.
they are some of the most positive, radiant people i
have ever met. they came to our wedding. . . we
will never forget!

and then there is my friend who bakes cinnamon
rolls. . . takes her children swimming. . . cries with
them. . . serves popcorn and hot cider by the
fireplace.
yet, the oldest child, a son — brilliant and a straight
"a" student — got involved in drugs.
his whole life went haywire. she and her
husband — good solid people — have watched
this child of huge potential deteriorate and

lose touch with any vision — almost with
   life itself.
there are tears. . .cries. . .prayers. . .trust.
but the clouds hang low. . .the heavy dark mist
   remains.

i have no solid answer. . .no crystal-clear formula.
does it seem too easy to say, "wait for God to work"?
my father prayed for thirty-one years for my brother
   to sincerely receive Christ into his life.
will waited thirty-seven years and prayed specifically
   for ten years, trusting God for
   His choice of a woman.
i faced many temptations and lonely times, waiting
   thirty-five years for this man.

pete and mary ellen stewart met in europe while both
   were involved with campus crusade for Christ.
they married and returned to the united states (peter
   was a native european) with a dream of pete's
   going to college and getting a degree.
when one starts a dream, one never knows what that
   dream will cost. how long it will take. how much
   courage it will entail. . .or what sacrifice and
   hardship.
one moves out with a sense of ecstasy and thrill over
   holding a fragile, wonderful vision.
in time the enthusiasm is chipped away by
   reality. . .by difficulty. . .by detours and
   roadblocks and long stretches of dark road.

before any of my dreams have actually lived, i have
   had to come to the place where i felt i was
   going to be crushed by opposition . . . by
   adversaries all around.
it has taken pete years to get his degree. meanwhile,
   three little boys were born into this home.
   beautiful children . . . but there was food and
   housing to provide. long hours of working.
   little boys often without a daddy around.
mary ellen, a professional woman when she
   married . . . now tied down to a small
   house . . . three incredibly active,
   not-always-easy-to-handle little boys.
   a husband gone much of the time . . .
   barely enough money to survive.
sometimes it takes a long time to see God at work.

will's sister julie and her husband, tom, have always
   had the dream of tom's becoming a country doctor.
his father and a brother were physicians. another
   brother is a dentist. the family's hearts all
   center around medicine.
tom has sent in applications to medical schools for
   eleven years . . . with over one hundred rejections.
weeks . . . months . . . years of going to the mailbox . . .
   either finding it empty or with another "no."
once in a while, being invited for an interview.
   hopes raised . . . spirits high . . .
   only to have the final decision be negative.

friends and family tend to shake their heads . . . to
   wonder if tom is not carried away with an
   unrealistic goal.

he keeps taking more science courses, earning more
  master's degrees. undeterred. uncompromising.
  waiting.
those who know tom personally realize this is an
  intelligent, disciplined, ordered, and godly man.
  not an extremist. not an egotist.
he is now thirty-eight years old.
they always knew it would take a miracle for all the
  pieces to fall into place, but they did not
  realize how *great* a miracle.

> *abraham, in hope, believed. . . he did not waver through
> unbelief regarding the promise of God, but was
> strengthened in his faith and gave glory to God,
> being fully persuaded that God had power to do
> what He had promised. . . . romans 4:20, 21.*

will tom eventually get into medical school?
is this, subconsciously, a human dream rather than a
  Divine one? only Jesus really knows.
i do know his and julie's hearts are right, and God will
  lead them to a specific place of His choosing.

one of the most powerful, moving books i have ever
  read is the autobiography of bishop fulton sheen,
  treasures in clay. in it he says,
  *i can remember when, after four months in the hospital,
    i began to recover; i was reading Mass on an altar
    constructed over the bed, before a few priests and friends.*
  *i said that i was glad i had open-heart surgery, because
    when the Lord comes to take us all, He will look to
    see if we have any marks of the Cross upon ourselves.*
  *He will look at our hands to see if they are crucified from
    sacrificial giving; He will look at our feet to see
    if they have been thorn-bruised and nail-pierced searching
    for lost sheep.*

*He will look at our heart to see if that has been opened
    to receive His Divine Heart.
    oh, what joy is mine just to have endured the minuscule
    imitation of His suffering on the Cross by having a
    wounded side.*

no. . .there are no easy, pat answers.
just a lot of questions tō ask Jesus when i see Him
    face to face.
bleeding, broken places. time to wait. . .
    maybe years and years.
but i will forever shout, "Jesus is love. . .
    and love, IF GIVEN TIME, turns *anything*
    into something beautiful and good."

a child encased in an ugly shell. . .but underneath,
    a heart so tough and radiant and brave that
    it breaks through the crust and ignites the world.
a child who could never have touched the world so
    powerfully except through the sorrow. . .for it is
    that very sorrow that teaches joel what love
    and feelings really are.

people living, still, with unanswered prayers. . .but
    believing. . .and while believing, turning softer
    and more mellow. . .refined. . .pure.
    more forgiving and compassionate.

will and i will tread some cold, numbing waters
    ahead. i know. . .that is life. that is real.
i have heard will pray, "Lord, the heat is on. . .but
    do not let up. i want to be Your man.
    WHATEVER it takes.
i have one life to live. teach me what you want me
    to be."

someday, Jesus will look to see the scars...the
wounds...the marks of cross-bearing.
He will recognize us and at the end of the race, we will
have won.
everything else will look very dim and insignificant
when we cross the finish line. we'll hear the
trumpets and the choirs...and only the face
of Jesus will matter.
we will be able to lay our burdens down.
the crippled will walk...the blind will see spring
flowers and distant mountains and the faces of
all they ever loved.
joel will have five fingers on each hand.
a large family will be reunited.
maybe i can run a fast marathon without pain!

questions will be forgotten. the pieces will fall into
place.
i will take your hand.
i will not have to tell you good-bye, or be rushed off
to another interview, or board another plane.

please...
wherever you are...
give God time.
never give up...never...never.
there is a new turn in the road for you...
a shining light at the end of the tunnel.
even now i can see it.

when Christ calls a man (woman), He bids him come and
die. in fact, every command of Jesus is the call
to die.
the call of discipleship means both death and life.
(bonhoeffer)
and the living is so wonderful!

glenn jenkins, will's number one man on the ranch . . . my friend. i send him surprises from my kitchen.

epilogue

from cultured, refined boston
   to idaho falls, idaho.
   40,000 population.
big sky, sage brush, diesel pumps on every block.
mountains on the horizon. no traffic jams.
men in cowboy boots. miles of potatoes and wheat.
   quiet streets. little pancake houses.
   horses and dogs and sheep.
homemade wheat bread and canning jars filled with
   stewed tomatoes and peaches and plums.
fresh chicken and the best beef on the table.
a customer can buy a bed or refrigerator in the
   morning. . .it is delivered that same afternoon.

cool nights. dry, clean air.
the silence of fields outside the windows.
hard workers. eternal dreamers.
   farmers waiting for next year's crops.
people molded by the seasons. . .the earth.

a full moon in a wide, endless sky.
   making faces. smiling.
cold, newborn morning air on my skin. . .
   crawling up my legs. making me shiver.

can i take your hand? or yours?
   or laugh over hot chocolate?
   or cry at your table?

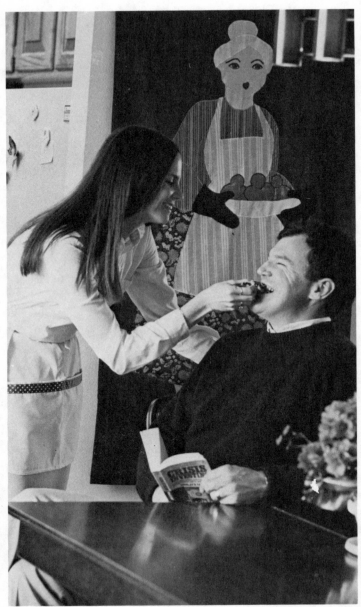

feeding my husband cookies.
(he loves them!)

honey, can i be your wife?
can i surprise you with an afternoon kiss . . .
    or a warm oatmeal cookie. can i?

being happy and contented in His plan.
doing His will with joy.
finding the song on the horizon.
    giving God room.
waiting until the music fills the sky . . .
    and the miracles live.

when one waits, the gift is more valuable . . .
    more priceless and cherished.
and God always knows when we are ready.

i gave God time . . .
and His plan was perfect.
it exceeded all my greatest expectations.

the Lord is wonderfully good to those
who wait for him, to those who seek for
him. it is good both to hope and wait
quietly for the salvation of the Lord.

lamentations 3:25, 26